THE ANCIENT NOVEL

An introduction

Niklas Holzberg

Translated by
Christine Jackson-Holzberg

London and New York

First published in German in 1986
by Artemis-Verlag

English translation first published 1995
by Routledge
11 New Fetter Lane, London EC4P 4EE

Simultaneously published in the USA and Canada
by Routledge
29 West 35th Street, New York, NY 10001

German edition © 1986 Artemis-Verlag, München und Zürich
English translation © 1995 Routledge

Typeset in Garamond by
Florencetype Ltd, Stoodleigh, Devon
Printed and bound in Great Britain by
Clays Ltd, St Ives PLC

British Library Cataloguing in Publication Data
A catalogue record for this book is available from the British Library

Library of Congress Cataloging in Publication Data
A catalogue record for this book has been requested

ISBN 0–415–10752–0 (hbk)
ISBN 0–415–10753–9 (pbk)

To Daniel Mackay

CONTENTS

CONTENTS

AUTHOR'S NOTE

This book was originally published in German in 1986. In the nine years since then, many new studies on various aspects of ancient prose fiction have been written, and research in this field has advanced considerably. A certain amount of revision and rewriting has therefore preceded the book's translation into English. The bibliography has been brought up to date and extended to include literature on the 'fringe novels', in which recent scholarship has shown particular interest.

Where ancient authors are quoted, the translation given here is in most cases the rendering found in B. P. Reardon (ed.), *Collected Ancient Greek Novels* (Berkeley/Los Angeles/London, 1989) or in the appropriate volumes of the Loeb Classical Library.

1

THE GENRE

Of all the television serials and dramas designed solely to entertain –
some commanding an audience as large as the readership of penny-
dreadfuls or romantic novelettes – perhaps the most spectacular in
terms of ratings over the past twenty to thirty years have been those
'soaps' which serialize the vicissitudes in the lives of the fabulously
wealthy. In the 1980s, for example, viewers all over the world
followed avidly the loves, lies and woes of American oil magnates
and millionaires: regular episodes full of romance, unscrupulous-
ness, intrigues, legal battles, dangerous journeys, devastating illness,
near death, families being reunited with relatives whom they had
believed dead or of whose existence they had been completely
unaware, and the obligatory happy ending for each calamity,
though with the next disasters coming thick and fast. The greater
part of the viewing public that consumes this type of entertainment
is probably unaware that the literature of ancient Greece, which is
generally thought of as high-brow in content and edifying rather
than entertaining, could offer readers something in many respects
remarkably similar: a goodly selection of fictional prose narratives.
Some of these are fully extant or survive in fragments, others are
now entirely lost. Their beginnings as a genre probably lie in the late
Hellenistic period, and they came into their prime in the first and
second centuries AD.

A conventional plot: Xenophon's *Ephesiaca*

The narrative components of these ancient novels bear a striking
resemblance to the motifs which together constitute a typical plot

for the kind of television soap opera described above, and an example of one such text will serve best as an introduction to a genre with which even many classical scholars are still unfamiliar. Particularly ample use of these stock motifs is made by Xenophon of Ephesus in his *Ephesiaca* ('An Ephesian Story').

The two central characters of this work are Habrocomes, a young Ephesian, and his slightly younger wife Anthia; the couple are separated shortly after their wedding and only after a long odyssey around the Mediterranean are they reunited and can settle down to live a happily married life. Habrocomes is an unusually handsome young man, intelligent, eminently capable and from a distinguished family. At the beginning of the novel he falls in love with the equally wonderful Anthia, the flames of passion being the punishment for an excessive pride in his own physical and mental qualities; this had led him to scorn Eros. The enraged god of love has him lose his heart to the 14-year-old Anthia at first sight – during a procession in honour of Artemis – and the girl is smitten with a similarly violent passion. Both suffer wretchedly for a while until their worried parents are informed of their children's love for each other by the oracle of Apollo at Colophon and accordingly decide that the two must marry. The oracle also makes obscure references to peregrinations and tribulations in store for the couple, but then to an eventual turn for the better in their fortunes. Considering it best to act upon these words, the parents send Habrocomes and Anthia off on a sea-journey not long after the wedding. The two pledge absolute fidelity at the outset and this is very soon put to the test. After a short stop at Rhodes, where Anthia and Habrocomes bring an offering of golden armour to the temple of the sun-god, their ship is attacked by pirates and the couple are carried off to the pirate captain's country home near the Phoenician city of Tyre; there the first mate takes a fancy to Habrocomes, while Anthia becomes the object of another pirate's passionate desires. The first of the five books of the novel ends on a note of deliberate suspense, much like an episode of any modern television serial: Habrocomes and Anthia have been advised of the pirates' respective love for them and ask for time to think things over, leaving the audience to wonder what the two will do in this predicament.

At the beginning of the second book the suspense is first heightened, with the couple deciding to commit suicide as a means of escaping the imminent danger, but then the pirate captain claims Habrocomes and Anthia as slaves for himself; he takes them with him to Tyre, together with Leucon and Rhode, hitherto the pair's own slaves. The captain's daughter Manto now falls in love with Habrocomes, is rejected even after several propositions and, in her disappointment, takes a revenge which leads to the separation of the couple. Like Joseph at the mercy of Potiphar's wife, Habrocomes is accused by Manto before her father of trying to rape her, is duly flogged and cast into prison; Manto is given in marriage to a Syrian, and Anthia, who has been passed on to her as a slave along with Leucon and Rhode, must accompany her mistress to her new home in Antioch. From this point onwards the story switches back and forth from Habrocomes to Anthia, describing their respective experiences in for the most part very short instalments; here again one is reminded of modern television serials where one episode consists of a succession of single scenes lasting often barely a minute. The rest of the second book alternates in six passages between Habrocomes and Anthia, with three for each. We are told how Anthia is forced by Manto to marry a goatherd who is, however, sympathetic to the girl's misery and does not lay a finger on her; how Manto's husband falls in love with Anthia, whereupon Manto orders the goatherd to kill the girl, but he again is moved by pity and sells her instead to Cilician merchants; how Anthia is shipwrecked on the way to Cilicia, captured by the robber Hippothous and his men, almost sacrificed by them to the god Ares, but rescued by Perilaus, a magistrate from Tarsus, during a raid on the robbers; how, finally, she is asked by Perilaus for her hand in marriage and is only able to negotiate a delay of thirty days for her answer. Whilst all this is going on, Habrocomes, his name cleared after only a brief spell in prison, is searching for his wife, but always arrives just a little too late. This (mis-)timing is throughout the novel an effective means of linking together a succession of adventures – a device, incidentally, also used in modern television serials. On his release Habrocomes learns from the goatherd himself of Anthia's unconsummated marriage with him and of her renewed enslavement; at the end of the second book he reaches Cilicia, where he meets with

3

and befriends the robber Hippothous, who had managed to escape during the raid on his band.

On the way to Cappadocia, where Hippothous hopes to recruit new men for his band, each of the two friends tells his life-story. In the robber's case this takes the form of a novella inserted by the author into the plot of the novel; it relates the tragic tale of Hippothous' love for a youth. Meanwhile, with the thirty-day postponement over, a suicidal Anthia procures poison from an Ephesian doctor, but after the burial she wakes up in her tomb, the potion having been a mere sleeping draught; grave-robbing pirates take her to Alexandria and sell her into slavery. Habrocomes sets out for the city not long after this, having heard about the plundered tomb and left Hippothous' company; in Egypt there now await further threats to the couple's mutual fidelity. Anthia, whose new master, an Indian, is making serious advances, is able to stall him for the moment by claiming that she had been dedicated to Isis at birth and must serve for one more year, while Habrocomes, who has been shipwrecked in the Nile Delta on his way to Alexandria, is sold by plunderers to an elderly army veteran in Pelusium, is propositioned by the old man's enamoured wife, but rejects her. At the end of the third book the wife kills her husband and Habrocomes, whom abhorrence for the deed moves to a final 'no!', is accused by her of the murder and brought before the prefect of Egypt in Alexandria.

The beginning of the fourth book prepares the ground for a third line of action which is to extend the plot of the novel: Hippothous has started to look for Habrocomes and after passing through Egypt he and his newly-formed band of robbers reach Ethiopia. Habrocomes has meanwhile been tied to a cross on the banks of the Nile and is praying in his distress to the sun-god; a sudden gust of wind knocks him into the river, but he is fished out at the delta and sentenced to death by fire; he is saved again, this time when the river overflows its banks, and the prefect puts him into prison until an explanation can be found for such miraculous happenings. The scene now changes briefly to Anthia and her fate, then back to Habrocomes, who is set free and decides to continue his search for Anthia in Italy. She meanwhile has been taken to Ethiopia as a member of the Indian's entourage and there she falls again into the hands of Hippothous, although neither recognizes the other; in the last episode of the fourth book her determination to remain a faithful wife is once more endangered by the advances of one of Hippothous' men; he tries to rape her and she kills him with a sword. For this she is thrown into a trench with two huge dogs, but is protected from them by another robber, who loves her and secretly feeds the animals.

The fifth and last book brings the protagonists of the three lines of action one after the other to Italy, although they are not actually reunited there; a fourth story-line is introduced by changing the scene to Rhodes for a while, where the two slaves Leucon and Rhode, the account of whose fate has been broken off in the second book and is now picked up again, have in the meantime been freed and are now rich. The first episode of the book deals with Habrocomes, who spends some time with an old fisherman in Syracuse and listens to the man's life-story, this taking the form of another inserted novella. After three episodes with Hippothous and three with Anthia, these alternating with each other, and after the start of the new story-line featuring Leucon and Rhode, we learn that Habrocomes has next gone to Nuceria in southern Italy and is earning his living as a quarry labourer. Hippothous has meanwhile moved to Egypt with his band and, after being once again the sole survivor of a raid, he sets sail for Sicily; the raid had been organized by Polyidus, a relative of Egypt's prefect, and Anthia, who has been rescued from her trench by the second of her robber admirers, soon falls into the hands of Polyidus. She escapes his advances by fleeing to the temple of Isis; an oracle tells her that she will shortly be reunited with Habrocomes, but for the moment she becomes the victim of Polyidus' jealous wife, who has her sold to a brothel-keeper in Tarentum. She is able to dodge her duties in his house by faking an epileptic fit, until at last – and we are told this immediately after the news of Habrocomes' quarry labouring – Hippothous, who in the meantime has married an old woman, inherited her fortune and come to Tarentum in the company of a young male beloved, sees the girl, recognizes her as Anthia and is told what has happened to her. In the following episodes Habrocomes, then Anthia and Hippothous arrive in Rhodes and all encounter Leucon and Rhode there.

In order to delay the imminent happy ending as long as possible, the author divides events in Rhodes into three recognition scenes. First, Habrocomes meets Leucon and Rhode in the temple of Helius beside a pillar which they had had erected next to Habrocomes and Anthia's earlier offering of golden armour and which was inscribed in memory of the couple. Secondly, Leucon and Rhode discover Hippothous and Anthia in the temple of Helius a day after finding there a lock of hair together with an inscription naming Habrocomes and his wife, an offering just brought by Anthia. Thirdly, Habrocomes hears of this reunion, runs through the city shouting 'Anthia!' and meets the others by the temple of Isis. They spend the rest of the day telling each other their stories and in the night Habrocomes and Anthia swear that neither has broken their former vow of fidelity; on the morrow they all return to Ephesus and live there together happily ever after.

The surviving texts

Written about the beginning of the second century AD, the *Ephesiaca* is both in its use of the narrative motifs we have just considered and in its narrative technique, which will be discussed later, quite clearly related to a number of other ancient works of prose fiction. The following is a list of such texts with, for the moment, details only of the authors, titles (or rather, in some cases, the titles generally used today), and of the manuscript history:

1. Fully extant in manuscripts from the Middle Ages are, in addition to Xenophon of Ephesus' *Ephesiaca*, the novels *Chaereas and Callirhoe* of Chariton, *Leucippe and Clitophon* of Achilles Tatius, *Daphnis and Chloe* of Longus, and Heliodorus' *Aethiopica* ('An Ethiopian Story'). These have survived in parchment codices which are comparable to modern books in their outward appearance. In ancient Greece and Rome all texts were originally written on papyrus rolls and, together with pieces of ancient parchment codices, numerous fragments of such rolls have been discovered over the past hundred years, most of them conserved in Egypt's desert sands. Finds from ancient novels

include portions of the above-named works of Chariton, Achilles Tatius and Heliodorus, and in addition:

2. Fragments of the novels *Ninus*, *Sesonchosis*, *Metiochus and Parthenope*, *Chione*, *Calligone* and *Herpyllis*, further of Lollianus' *Phoenicica* ('A Phoenician Story') and other smaller remnants, the contents of which can barely be ascertained; the classification of these unidentified pieces as the type of narrative prose under discussion here is in any case dubious. Over and above these there have survived from the Middle Ages:

3. Summaries of the contents of two lost novels: *Ta huper Thoulen apista* ('The Wonders Beyond Thule') of Antonius Diogenes, and Iamblichus' *Babyloniaca* ('A Babylonian Story'). Fragments of both from ancient and medieval times also still exist.

An affinity to the type of novel represented by the texts listed above is found in four other novels. These use essentially the same narrative technique as the others, but in their narrative motifs they clearly parody the themes treated there. Probably the oldest of the four is the Latin text *Satyrica* ('A Story from the Land of the Satyrs') of Petronius, which survives only in medieval extracts and fragments. In Greek we have a fragment of the novel *Iolaus* and, further, the so-called *Ass Romance* in an abridged version falsely ascribed to Lucian; this epitome is entitled *Loukios e Onos* ('Lucius or the Ass'). The fourth of the texts is the Latin *Metamorphoses* of Apuleius, which is better known as *The Golden Ass*, the title given to it by St Augustine.

In the *Ass Romance*, to give an example, the place occupied in novels of the same type as the *Ephesiaca* by two lovers is taken by a young man who has been changed into an ass. His experiences are either represented as a comic distortion of the usual adventures undergone elsewhere by the two lovers – he is once faced, for instance, not with death, but castration – or they are depicted in a harshly realistic manner. Such variations immediately raise one question: do these four 'comic-realistic' novels with their unmistakably parodic features belong to the same genre as the above-listed novels with their idealizing representation of real life? This, in turn, leads us to the very difficult problem of finding a definition for the literary form 'ancient novel', a task which is further complicated by the fact that the relevant handbooks generally include under this heading other types of narrative prose fiction, such as 'utopian novel' or 'epistolary novel'. These are in some respects akin to the two kinds of novel named above in their subject-matter and narrative technique, but are in other respects also quite different. Ancient literary critics, moreover, are of little help here, because the treatises from late antiquity that deal with questions of literature see no need to discuss narrative prose fiction, indeed they do not even have a name for it. The terms 'novel', 'romance', *Roman*, etc., were coined at a much later date. 'Romance' is derived from the medieval French word used to describe longer verse or prose narratives written not in the language of the scholars, Latin, but in the vernacular, i.e. a Romance tongue. 'Novel' – first used in its present sense in the seventeenth century – comes from the Italian term *novella*, a short story of the ('new') type written by Boccaccio in his *Decameron*.

Ancient labels

The reason why ancient literary theorists, otherwise at pains to find comprehensive definitions for most other literary forms, ignored the novel is doubtlessly that they did not count it as true 'literature'. Fortunately we have passing references to the subject, dating in Greek from the Byzantine period and in Latin even from late antiquity; these serve as a kind of substitute terminology and do suggest that at least a certain group of longer fictional prose narratives was associated with a fairly specific type of story in terms of content. Where such texts are mentioned, they are called *drama*, (*suntagma*) *dramatikon* ('dramatic narrative') or *komodia* in Greek and *fabula* or *mimus* in Latin. Ancient readers clearly felt reminded by the tales told in the novels of stories staged in drama, and there are two very good reasons for this. First, the structure of some of Euripides' later tragedies and, more especially, of all extant comedies by Menander, Plautus and Terence is dictated by the tangled fortunes of two lovers happily joined together only at the end of the work, much the same as in novels like the *Ephesiaca*. Secondly, one important criterion in ancient definitions of 'comedy' is its realistic content. Epic poets and tragedians adapt material taken from mythology and thus from the realm of fantasy, far removed from reality; historians, by contrast, record real happenings. These two very different processes are in a manner combined in comedy, because the author there invents his stories, but deliberately makes them seem very true to life. Such fictional reproduction of everyday life in the ancient world is something also found in the novels mentioned above. In its broadest sense the term *suntagma drama-tikon* – one most probably already in use in late antiquity – means 'fictional narrative depicting the kind of everyday life otherwise portrayed in comedy'.

Characteristics of the idealistic and comic-realistic novels

Given these paraphrastic labels, it may be inferred that for a certain type of prose narrative a certain type of story was not only antici-pated by the readers, but was also automatically visualized a priori by the authors themselves. In their case such fixed notions meant that, within the framework of the story, their choice both of individual motifs and of the various devices by which these were to be represented invariably followed an almost stereotype pattern. Its outlines can even still be traced in the works of novelists who deviated from or played on it in some way. The mere presence of elements which are recurrent in all examples of this literary form itself also provides a basis for our attempt to define the genre. The following, therefore, is a list of such invariables, described for present purposes as they appear in their original form, i.e. in the idealistic novels exemplified above in our consideration of Xenophon's *Ephesiaca*.

1. *Motifs*: The main characters in the story are a young man and a young girl from distinguished families and of incomparable beauty; either as newly-weds or after their betrothal they set out on a long journey to far-off lands and undergo, together or separately, a series of in the main harrowing experiences. The most frequent cause of their tribulations is a mutual pledge of unswerving fidelity. Their strict observance of this puts them in peril when they fall into the hands of pirates or robbers or become slaves in the service of rich masters or mistresses. They are frequently in danger of being murdered or, with their backs to the wall for some other reason,

they decide in their desperation to kill themselves, only to be saved at the last minute or die merely an apparent death, which itself leads to further complications. The favoured setting for these adventures is Asia Minor and the Near East, where the couple meet not only with fellow-countrymen, but also with exotic strangers. When they are travelling by sea, the two are usually shipwrecked in a storm. At the end of their ordeals they are reunited and return home to live thereafter a life of complete bliss. On occasion there are one or more deities at work; these vent, for example, their wrath – as once in the *Odyssey* – after some misdemeanour on the part of the hero and/or the heroine, and thus trigger off a series of adventures.

2. *Narrative technique*: In deliberate imitation of the only other comparable form of prose representation in existence when ancient novels first began to appear, namely of historiographical texts, the author, like the historian, presents the action chronologically or relates the respective adventures of the separated protagonists in parallel accounts. Similarly he inserts at times short, novella-like stories about the experiences of other characters, or adds digressions, for instance on mythology or on a particular branch of learning. More complicated devices such as first-person narration, flashbacks or the gradual unravelling of tales within the tales – techniques which depart from the means of representation used in historiography, but which are all the more common in modern novel writing – only appear at a later stage in the development of the ancient novel. However, those techniques used by all authors of this genre are throughout – in the first as in the last surviving texts – a conscious imitation of historiographical methods. One particularly simple manifestation of this is in many cases the very title of the novel: *Ephesiaca*, *Phoenicica*, *Babyloniaca* and *Aethiopica* (further titles of this type are documented for lost novels or can be inferred for surviving texts). These are names which historiographers too might have chosen for their works, one very famous example from the Classical period being Xenophon of Athens' *Hellenica* ('Greek History'). The individual episodes of the ancient novel, on the other hand, are modelled on typical comedy and tragedy scenes. Once again we are reminded of modern television serials: long dialogues often take the place of the author's own narrative for considerable stretches, and frequent monologues and speeches reinforce the

dramatic quality of events, these culminating in many cases in a court-room scene.

The same narrative devices are used in the comic-realistic novels and these can therefore, in formal and aesthetic respects at least, claim an uncontested place in the history of the ancient novel. In terms of content and motifs they stand apart in so far as they substitute comic or realistic description for idealistic presentation of fictional reality: love-scenes of the kind which cannot take place in novels like the *Ephesiaca* because of their obligatory pledge of fidelity, are described in graphic detail in Petronius, the *Ass Romance*, and Apuleius, and were probably also found in *Iolaus*. None the less, the basis for the plot here too is love and predominantly harrowing experiences. Moreover, the final scene in the comic-realistic novels, or at least in the *Ass Romance* and *The Golden Ass* – we do not know how the *Satyrica* and *Iolaus* ended – is a happy one for the hero, as in the idealistic novels, and all four works could be called a *suntagma dramatikon*, since the world in which their protagonists live is that of everyday life. Finally, a comparison of the general outlook mirrored in both types of novel will show that they also share a certain ideological framework. The early Greek novels, as we shall see, reflect their authors' attitudes towards the particular social and political situation of their age. And the way in which the authors of the comic-realistic novels react to the picture of life drawn in those idealistic novels bears the unmistakable marks of an ideological dispute.

The fringe: other novel-like literature of antiquity

Both of these novel types can, then, be placed in the same category of ancient fiction and it is this genre alone that is to be the subject of the next chapters. Before attempting to sum up our findings so far in the form of a full definition, we must first let the so-called 'fringe novels' pass review and show why any classification of these together with the idealistic and comic-realistic novels under one generic heading must be considered problematical. The two latter types of novel correspond closely to each other in their outward form, plot, motifs, and even in their ideology, if only in the sense that the one's is reversed in the other's. In the texts now to be

11

discussed, however, we shall encounter in every case only partial likenesses.

1. Utopia and fantastic travel

The motif 'journey to far-off lands' as found in the idealistic novels forms a link between these and two narratives in which the respective authors describe their journey to islands lying beyond the known world. The texts in question are known to us only in the form of summaries and fragments. 'Euhemerus of Messene' was the name used by the first-person narrator in the earlier of these two fictional reports, and he purported to have made several journeys abroad in the service of King Cassander of Macedon (305–297 BC). The contents of his account, the *Hiera anagraphe* ('The Sacred Inscription'), are summarized by Diodorus Siculus (first century BC) in his *Bibliotheca historica* (5.41–46; 6.1). On one of his trips, we are told, Euhemerus visited a group of islands of which the largest was called Panchaea and was in two respects a very remarkable place. It could, first, boast a magnificent temple dedicated to Zeus, standing in idyllic surroundings on unusually fertile land; inside it was a column inscribed with the history of the Greek gods and their cult. Zeus and the other Olympians were, according to this, originally mere mortals, kings who had been deified posthumously on account of their contributions to the civilization of man. Secondly, the island's social structure, which Euhemerus must have described at considerable length, displayed primitive communistic features.

The author of the other island narrative is cited by Diodorus as one 'Iambulus', a merchant who had been travelling through Arabia when he was taken prisoner first by brigands, then by Ethiopians; the latter sent him and a companion off to a 'blessed isle'. This too – writes Diodorus (2.55–60) – was an earthly paradise in terms of climate and fertility, and the social order amongst the inhabitants was, like that of the Panchaeans, characterized by principles of primitive communism. Other wonders found by Diodorus in Iambulus had for the most part to do with the physical attributes of the islanders and of the animal population; the blood of a tortoise-like creature, for example, could be used to re-affix severed limbs.

Both of these narratives have repeatedly been defined as utopian novels and, consequently, ancient forerunners of Thomas More's classic work. Moreover, it has frequently been the automatic assumption that the framework in which Euhemerus and Iambulus each embedded their respective island descriptions took the form of a travel novel. In the case of *The Sacred Inscription*, however, this is pure speculation. Diodorus' brief reference to the 'official' nature of Euhemerus' travels could just as easily represent a similarly brief remark to this effect in the original narrative, where the words could simply have been meant to help pass off the picture he draws of the island as a true account of facts. The author's main purpose would then have been to present this very description and combine it with an outline of the island's political constitution, proffering all this as an ideal state. Iambulus, on the other hand, described how he came to land on his island and how he later returned to Greece, travelling through India and Persia and, as the *Bibliotheca* tells us, meeting with a number of further adventures along the way. If his account of the island takes up most of the space allotted him by Diodorus, then the probable reason for this is that the historian was interested solely in the *mirabilia* of an exotic civilization that only Iambulus had put down in writing. This would also explain why Diodorus' account seems to jump confusingly from one theme to another, back and forward from 'life-style of the islanders' to 'social structure', 'flora and fauna', etc. The first-person narrator in the original described the island phenomena in the order in which he himself was on varying occasions confronted with them, and Diodorus simply omitted the circumstances leading to each observation. There are, therefore, no grounds for the assumption that the description of the island formed the central theme of Iambulus' original narrative and was intended, like Euhemerus' account, as the systematic representation of a socio-political ideal. Thus only *The Sacred Inscription* can with a certain degree of probability be regarded as a forerunner of modern utopian novels, while Iambulus' chief intention will have been to offer a colourful account of his strange experiences on a trip away from home.

Whatever the case, the existence of at least one Hellenistic travel novel would seem to be beyond question. Whether the adventures undergone by this protagonist in far-off lands were narrated in a form comparable to the way in which the experiences of the heroes and heroines in novels like Xenophon's *Ephesiaca* were presented, is impossible to say. The only knowledge we have of the outward appearance of Iambulus' narrative is derived from a distortive caricature drawn by Lucian of Samosata (*c.* 120–180). In the two books of his *Alethe diegemata* ('True Stories') Lucian parodies the accounts written by various Greek authors – amongst them Iambulus – of the *mirabilia* to be found in exotic civilizations. Since most of these accounts are now no longer extant, we can have but an inkling of the wit and deeper meaning of much of this literary satire. The series of adventures experienced by the first-person narrator is none the less highly entertaining and amusing. They take place on the moon with the Horse-vultures, Millet-slingers, Sunites, Moonites, then in the belly of a whale, on a sea of ice, on a sea of milk with an island made of cheese, amongst the Corkfeet, on the Isle of the Blest, the Isles of the Wicked and in the City of Dreams, amongst the Pumpkin-pirates, Nut-sailors, Bullheads, Phallonauts and Asslegs. But this is quite definitely a world which is only very faintly reminiscent of the settings chosen for the idealistic and comic-realistic novels of antiquity.

2. *Fictional biography*

The list of texts defined by us as ancient novels proper includes two titles which represent a particular subcategory within the genre, *Ninus* and *Sesonchosis*. The heroes of these two fragmentary novels are actual historical figures, both famous kings who reigned in the East long before the rise of Greece. By analogy, histories of literature have generally tended to attach the label 'novel' to four ancient works which each describe the life of a great man: to Xenophon of Athens' *vita* of Cyrus, King of Persia (*Cyropaedia*), to the anonymous *Life of Aesop*, to Pseudo-Callisthenes' *Life and Deeds of Alexander of Macedon*, and to Philostratus' *Life of Apollonius of Tyana*. In so far as the historical core in each of these four works is almost totally obscured by a mantle of fiction, this designation may be considered justifiable. There is, however, one essential difference between the four 'novels' with historical personages as protagonists and the two named above. As the fragments we shall be looking at clearly show, the plot in these latter two rests, like the plot of the *Ephesiaca*, on a quite specific set of adventures undergone by the protagonist; these arise once again from his unswerving fidelity to a beloved and take the form of shipwreck, separation, animosities, etc. In the other four works, however, the plot covers the life of the protagonist from birth to death, and fictionalization is not the recipe for the narrative, but simply one ingredient. It is used to add a particular quality to the biography of a famous person, the *vita* being designed either to serve a didactic purpose or to entertain an audience with no taste for dry historical facts, or to do both.

In the eight books of his *Cyropaedia* ('Education of Cyrus'), the Athenian historian Xenophon (*c.* 425–355 BC) draws the novel-like portrait of a consummate monarch, deliberately changing the biographical facts and inventing new ones in order to make his Persian king a model of royal excellence. We see Cyrus being trained to become a military leader who goes on to conquer the peoples of Asia campaign by campaign; at the same time we are shown how he matures into a benevolent ruler. The events of his childhood and adult life reported here are for the most part fictional and merely form a setting for the proof of his numerous virtues. The 'novel' content of the work is, then, primarily designed as a mirror of princeliness in narrative form, although the story does include one incidental tale which bears some resemblance to the plot of a typical idealistic romance. This is a novella related in intermittent episodes and spread over a lengthy stretch of the text. It tells the tale of Panthea's conjugal fidelity which, put to the test, remains unfailing; in the end she commits suicide over the corpse of Abradatas, the husband slain in battle. It was quite probably this account that provided the first authors of Greek novels with one of their central thematic inspirations for the genre; more will be said of this in the next chapter. For the moment we must only note that the part played by the *Cyropaedia* in the genre 'ancient novel' is restricted to this very loose genetic link.

What Xenophon was basically doing in his fictional biography of Cyrus was teaching by telling a story. Other Greek authors before and after him used a similar device for the same end – the insertion of a fable, be it into verse, into rhetorical texts or into historiographical works. The anonymous second- or third-century author of the *Bios tou Aisopou* ('Life of Aesop') even went so far as to base the entire *vita* on a structural pattern frequently used in fables. His description of the events which lead to the murder of Aesop by the Delphian priests is clearly influenced in its structure by the type of fable which tells its story in three phases: someone does something right, then something wrong, and so, finally, brings about his own end. The murder of Aesop is a motif which can be traced back to sources from the fifth century BC, and our anonymous author's version of the circumstances surrounding the bloody deed is as follows: Aesop is a mute in the first part of the *vita*, but is able to foil a plot against him by using the appropriate gesticulations; shortly afterwards the Muses reward him for a pious action with the gift of eloquence. In the central part of the *vita* he uses his newly acquired talent first as a slave in the household of the philosopher Xanthus, where it brings him his freedom, and then as adviser to the people of Samos and to the king of Babylon, where it brings him honours and wealth. At the end of this section, however, he has a temple erected for the Muses as thanks for their gift and raises in the midst of their statues not a likeness of Apollo Musegetes, but of himself; with this he incurs the wrath of the god. In the third part of the story Aesop is in Delphi, where Apollo encourages his priests in their conspiracy against the fabulist and thus endorses the murder.

The moral of the tale is clear: for the silver-tongued too, pride comes before a fall. The man who was once able to save his skin simply by miming is now, by contrast, powerless to help himself, even though in the face of execution he brings his special skill to the fore – he tells fables and, in doing so, he argues in narrative like an orator. It is scarcely the simple moral that creates the particular appeal of this novel-like *vita*, but rather the contents of the various episodes prior to Aesop's death. Many of them are clearly reminiscent of scenes from picaresque novels. On the one hand they tell of wily tricks played by the rogue protagonist and, on the other, the exposure of discrepancies between appearances and reality is a central theme. The proximity to Petronius' *Satyrica* and the Greek *Onos* is evident.

Popular narratives of the same type as *The Life of Aesop* were not always handed down in the original wording in antiquity and the Middle Ages. Their language and contents were often revised, and extended or abridged versions were created in the process. It was the most widely known of the fictional biographies written in antiquity that was subjected to the most changes of this kind: the three books of a third-century narrative falsely ascribed to the Hellenistic historian Callisthenes (*c.* 370–327 BC) and entitled *Bios kai praxeis Alexandrou tou Makedonou* ('Life and Deeds of Alexander of Macedon'). The manuscript tradition numbers at least five recensions; these are supplemented by Julius Valerius' Latin version (*c.* 300) and translations into a number of languages (e.g. Armenian), these renderings possibly having been based on further recensions of the original. The textual history is so complicated that scholarly work on what is known as the *Alexander Romance* has so far barely progressed beyond attempts to reconstruct the original, the history of its transmission and its sources. And we can safely shelve the conclusions reached in this line of study, because the methods used have, even in quite recent times, been those of nineteenth-century historicism, an approach which cannot be regarded with sufficient scepticism from a modern point of view.

If one simply takes a look at recension A, which is generally held to be the oldest, one soon perceives that the great king is, like Aesop, at many points in the *vita* best compared to protagonists of novels such as Petronius' *Satyrica*. One significant explanation for this at first somewhat surprising characterization could be the fact that Pseudo-Callisthenes, unlike the historians, is not primarily interested in Alexander's military achievements, choosing instead to portray him as a sort of wandering adventurer. He even lets him relate through his own mouth his experiences abroad, for example in a long letter which Alexander writes to his former preceptor Aristotle describing the wonders of India (3.17), an account which is reminiscent of Diodorus' rendering of Iambulus' 'eye-witness' report. With an Alexander such as this it is then quite in character that in the few situations where the reader would expect him to prove his worth as a prince, he behaves like a picaresque hero. In a duel with the much taller King Porus of India, for example, Alexander only manages to defeat his opponent because he can turn one brief moment in which the other is distracted by a sudden noise to his own advantage, deftly dealing the final blow with his sword (3.4). This and similar scenes can scarcely raise an eyebrow in a *vita* which has Alexander's mother Olympias conceive her son not with her husband King Philip of Macedon, but with the Egyptian king and sorcerer Nectanebus, who tricks and conjures his way into her bed (1.1–12). However, classical scholars whose image of Alexander is taken from the biographies written by historians will doubtlessly need some time before they are ready to acknowledge that Pseudo-Callisthenes' fictional narrative too is a literary text following a specific design.

The last of the fictional biographies under discussion here, *Ta es ton Tuanea Apollonion* ('Life of Apollonius of Tyana') was written in the early third century by the Neosophist Philostratus. Its subject is a Pythagorean magician whose existence is documented for the first century. His *vita* is presented here as a series of pious deeds performed by an ascetic sage. Teaching and preaching virtue, Apollonius travels across the entire eastern and western Mediterranean world, going on to India, Egypt and Ethiopia. On his way he works numerous wonders such as prophesying, exorcism, healing the sick and wakening a dead girl. He also experiences a variety of adventures which on a few occasions call to mind motifs used in the idealistic and comic-realistic novels. Furthermore, the *vita* is particularly closely akin to the later Greek novels of Iamblichus, Achilles Tatius and Heliodorus in that it contains frequent geographical and scientific digressions on the flora and fauna of the far-off lands visited by Apollonius. The work was primarily intended as edification and Pythagorean religious propaganda (the author claims that it was commissioned by Julia Domna, the wife of Emperor Septimius Severus) and it remains, in spite of the above-mentioned similarities, far removed from being a 'novel'. This said, we do find here, for the first time in our survey of 'fringe' texts, something remotely comparable in the general tenor. The underlying idea of this *vita* is undoubtedly that a wise, just and pious life, as exemplified in the behaviour of the holy man, can deliver from all manner of danger anywhere in the world. This is a theme which has parallels not only in the Christian novel-like literature to be discussed later in this survey (see pp. 22–6), but also, after a fashion, in the early Greek novels, as we shall see in Chapter 2. The certainty there that for two unswervingly faithful lovers subjected to bitter suffering final happiness is in store can be interpreted as a sort of profane doctrine of salvation.

3. Historical novels in epistolary form

Related in content to the fictional biographies are those collections of pseudepigraphic letters which reflect a specific series of events in the life of the first-person writer, the epistles being arranged for this purpose in chronological order. The known collections of this kind were written in Greek only, as were originally the novel-like biographies too. The oldest corpus, one which was possibly already in existence in its extant form around 200 BC, is most probably that of the letters of Plato. Although the one or the other of these epistles may even be genuine, the collection itself none the less forms an integral whole, in the first half of which the writer looks back and retraces his experiences at the court of Dionysius II, tyrant of Syracuse. The other collections, which all centre on and, as it were, serialize a particular biographical episode, were, with one exception, written in the late Hellenistic and early Imperial ages. It is certain that they contain no genuine letters of the historical personages in question, these being Themistocles, Euripides, Socrates and the Socratics, Hippocrates, Chion of Heraclea and Aeschines. A collection bearing the name of the Sicilian tyrant Phalaris was probably not written until the fourth century and also differs from the others in that it does not reflect one sequence of events; it offers instead merely letters which can be grouped together on the basis of thematic links. A number of letters inserted by Diogenes Laertius (third century) into his history of philosophy can be joined together to reconstruct the pseudepigraphic correspondence of the 'Seven Wise Men'. Lastly, there is evidence of the possible existence of a corpus that contained chronologically arranged letters under the name of Alexander the Great, if the interpretation given by Reinhold Merkelbach to a second-century papyrus is correct.

These collections can quite clearly be classed as ancient forerunners of modern epistolary novels, but have as such only recently begun to arouse interest amongst classical scholars. After the publication in 1697 of Richard Bentley's famous essay on the *Phalaris Letters*, in which he exposed the epistles – previously held to be genuine – as 'forgeries', this kind of epistolography was thenceforth generally dismissed and only the question of authenticity occasionally deemed worthy of consideration. And yet all of these historical 'novels' in epistolary form have a narrative structure as composite and united as that of other Greek works of prose fiction. We only need to look, for example, at the story unfolded in the pseudepigraphic letters of Hippocrates. Instead of accepting King Artaxerxes' invitation to go to Persia, the physician travels to Abdera at the request of its citizens; they want him to cure Democritus, whom they believe to be out of his mind because he laughs all the time. The two hold a long conversation in which Democritus talks much of the insanity of men's actions – madness being the subject of a book he is currently writing – and Hippocrates realizes that the other is in fact the greatest of sages. One particularly novel-like feature of this corpus is the suspense built up in seven letters preceding the physician's arrival in Abdera.

While nine of the pseudepigraphic collections named above are associated with famous figures, the author of the *Letters of Chion* chose as his writer a man who, even for contemporary readers then, was probably not very familiar. The historical Chion had assassinated the Heraclean tyrant Clearchus in the year 353–352 BC, and by early Imperial times little more was known about him than this one fact. The anonymous author of the 'epistolary novel' was therefore able to portray the protagonist and his story with a greater degree of poetic licence than was permissible for the other authors of pseudepigraphic letters. This freedom is used to mirror in the letters an inner, cognitive development. Chion writes the first letter while on his way to Athens to study under Plato, and the last (of a total of seventeen) when back in Heraclea, on the day before the assassination of Clearchus. Over the period covered by the letters Chion gradually matures to become a 'good man' in an ethical sense and at the same time a responsible citizen. These processes are conveyed to us in the words of a 'first-person narrator', in a form, then, which represents a clear connection between the *Letters of Chion* and other epistolary 'novels' on the one hand, and Petronius' *Satyrica*, the Greek *Onos*, Apuleius' *Metamorphoses* and Achilles Tatius' *Leucippe* on the other. In the latter four works, of course, the 'I' of the story is a purely fictional character, whilst Chion and the others are historical figures. Presenting as they do a particular period of the protagonist's life through his own eyes, the *Letters of Chion* and other texts of this type could even be styled a blend of fictional *auto*biography and first-person narrative.

4. *Fictional reports from Troy*

We have already touched upon the transposition of history into fiction in *Ninus* and *Sesonchosis*, where famous, bona fide rulers become the heroes of invented stories, and in the next chapter we shall be discussing what role such combinations of fact and fiction could have played in the genesis of the ancient novel. For the present, however, it must be noted that ancient narrative literature includes one type of text in which the method used in *Ninus* and *Sesonchosis* is, as it were, reversed. In the so-called 'Troy novels' fictional events from mythology are presented as genuine historical happenings. It is tempting to believe that the first novel-like venture of this kind was made in the early second century BC by Hegesianax of Alexandria in his *Troïka* ('Stories from Troy'), but the only extant fictional reports from Troy date from Imperial times and are written in Latin. One is the *Ephemeris belli Troiani* ('Diary of the Trojan War') written by a 'Greek eye-witness', Dictys Cretensis (probably fourth century), and the other the *Historia de excidio Troiae* ('History of the Destruction of Troy') by a 'Trojan eye-witness', Dares Phrygius (before the end of the fifth century). Traces of a Greek original of the *Ephemeris* from the first/second century have survived in papyrus fragments, and it seems fairly probable that the *Historia* too was based on an earlier Greek version.

In both of these texts the picture drawn of the Trojan War presents a marked deviation from traditional mythology as first found in the Homeric epics; thus both in Dictys and in Dares the gods play no part in the affair. Recent studies have interpreted such radical divergence from the familiar versions of the various battle situations as a literary game. At first glance this seems implausible, the style of both texts being unsophisticated, that of Dares even quite primitive. However, a closer look shows that the absence of elegant diction is deliberately intended as part of an elaborate attempt to give the text credibility as a historical document. This means that we must expect to find some degree of artifice and contrivance. Much the same as Caesar in his account of the Gallic Wars, the two alleged veterans use a plain and strictly factual style, reporting throughout not in the first, but in the third person. And their writings are both 'rediscovered' under extraordinary circumstances, as we are told in the preliminaries: the *Ephemeris* turns up in a grave and the *Historia* is found by a visitor to Athens, 'Cornelius Nepos', no less, who then writes the attached letter of dedication to 'Sallust'.

Such authenticating devices or, in a word, *Beglaubigungsapparate* are, as we shall see, also used in several idealistic novels; thus there is a clear link between the reports from Troy and the novels proper. Another more significant feature, one already observed in the *Alexander Romance*, reinforces this: traditionally heroic figures are again dislodged from their pedestals. The author of the *Ephemeris* has Hector, for example, killed not in open combat, but in an ambush (3.15). The grand struggles of the god-like and valiant are reduced to average battlefield skirmishes between quite ordinary men. In pseudo-historical texts this produces an effect which is not so far removed from that of a comic device found again and again in novels of the same type as Petronius' *Satyrica*: parodic play on heroic poses and false pathos. However, the disparity between Dictys and Dares on the one side, and the surviving comic-realistic novels of antiquity on the other is so great that any thought of ascribing all to the same genre seems particularly misplaced.

5. Early Christian novel-like literature

It has frequently been noted that the canonical *Acts of the Apostles* contain thematic parallels to ancient novels: journeys fraught with peril, last-minute rescue, court-room scenes, and a shipwreck (chapter 27). In his depiction of those of the apostles' experiences that resemble situations typical for the novel, St Luke clearly used a technique and style calculated to remind his audience of similar scenes in narrative fiction. He could then expect the type of reader most likely to have enjoyed such texts to be all the more willing to read his work. The anonymous authors of the various apocryphal

Acts, which first appeared in the second century and were especially popular in the third, increased considerably the thematic similarities to 'secular' novels; they even introduced the love motif, albeit in a modified form. Thus they undeniably created a new type of fictional prose narrative which can in a certain sense quite legitimately be labelled the 'early Christian novel'. However, they cannot be included in the genre 'ancient novel', because they represent more properly the beginnings of its reception and influence. The variations on the theme of the lovers beset by misfortunes demonstrate alone that here the ideological climate has undergone a radical change. The place of the two lovers sworn to undying fidelity is taken by the apostle and a young woman who, on hearing him preach, converts on the spot to the new faith and thus to the love of Christ alone; whether already betrothed to another, married, or still single, she now pledges absolute chastity. The tribulations of the two are the result of their persecution on the part of a society still labouring under pagan delusions and unable to tolerate a form of continence which, to its mind, far exceeds the acceptable measure. Both the convert and the man who encourages such behaviour are accordingly faced with fire and sword. The story of Paul and Thecla as told in the *Praxeis* ('Acts') of Paul is the most exhaustive and most frequently imitated elaboration of these motifs.

What we have here is quite obviously a continuation and conversion of the late Hellenistic 'profane ideology of salvation' which we shall be discussing more fully below (see p. 30). The earthly happy ending that follows a long odyssey is now substituted by the heavenly joys which await the troubled 'couple'. However, it is equally obvious that this transposition takes the texts beyond the bounds set by a literary tradition which had risen out of a specific socio-political situation and then grown under circumstances which remained comparable. There is, finally, one more argument for the exclusion of early Christian novels from a discussion of the ancient genre. It is a consideration which departs somewhat from the approach we have taken so far towards a definition, this being based purely on the facts of ancient literature; nevertheless it ought to carry no little weight. The beginnings of the modern novel in the sixteenth and seventeenth centuries were, where the authors looked to ancient novels for inspiration, influenced solely by the pagan idealistic type (in particular by Heliodorus' *Aethiopica*) and its comic-realistic counterpart (especially the Greek and Latin *Ass* novels).

Amongst the early Christian novel texts there are two which would, more than any others, merit closer inspection within a history of the ancient novel, their adaptation of familiar motifs betraying as it does noticeable traces of the transition from the earlier to the later form of the novel. These are the so-called *Clement Romance* and the *Historia Apollonii regis Tyri* ('Story of Apollonius King of Tyre'). Their inclusion would, however, first necessitate an attempt to reconstruct the original pagan versions of both novels and that, in turn, would entail a lengthy and profound discussion of the contrary scholarly views on the matter. All of this would without a doubt go beyond the scope of an introduction such as ours, and we shall therefore restrict ourselves here, as in the case of the 'fringe novels' considered above, to a brief look at the two texts.

The *Clement Romance* is the fictional autobiography of the Apostle Peter's successor as Bishop of Rome; its two surviving parts are commonly known as the 'Pseudo-Clementines'. We have two fourth-century versions: the Greek *Homiliai* ('Sermons') and the *Recognitiones*, which are extant only in Rufinus of Aquileia's Latin translation. The respective writers are both more interested in defending the Christian faith than in rendering the original plot of the novel, but they differ, as the titles themselves suggest, in their dosing of theologically instructive passages, so that we learn more about the experiences of the future bishop in the *Recognitiones* than in the *Homiliai*. It is the fate of his family – his parents and two brothers have been drifting lost around the Mediterranean since he was a child – that forms the close thematic link between this and the novels of the same type as Xenophon's *Ephesiaca*. After a series of adventures (shipwreck, capture by pirates, etc.) the various members of the family are reunited one after the other with Clement, who has in the meantime become a follower of the Apostle Peter.

The substitution of blood relatives for the traditional pair of lovers need not necessarily point to a Christian modification of the motif, because in the *Historia Apollonii regis Tyri*, where the Christian element plays no very significant role, we find a similar constellation of characters. Surviving in two Latin versions from the fifth/sixth century, the text tells of the adventures of King Apollonius, his (unnamed) wife and their daughter Tarsia. He loses his wife while on board a ship – she is pronounced dead after giving birth and is buried at sea – and decides after this to leave the baby Tarsia for a life as a travelling merchant. Fourteen years later he is reunited with her in Mytilene where the girl, who has in the meantime been brought up by a nurse, kidnapped and sold into slavery by pirates, is managing to retain her virginity in spite of being owned by a brothel-keeper. An angel appears to Apollonius in a dream and tells him to go to Ephesus; there he finds the wife he had believed dead serving as priestess in the temple of Diana.

The curious alliance of Christian and pagan elements is visible even in this very condensed summary of the contents. There is another distinctive feature of the narrative which only a more detailed outline of the plot would bring to the fore. The story consists of a medley of episodes which are complete in themselves, but which are not linked together with the stringent coherence one might expect of a novel's plot; occasionally they even seem to contradict one another. The general consensus of opinion today is, therefore, that the extant texts of the *Historia*, both written in late antiquity and neither differing significantly from the other, merely represent an abridged version of the tale. Attempts to reconstruct the lost original could perhaps be facilitated by two papyri which date from the third century and contain fragments of a Greek prose text. They offer a scene in which an Apollonius appears before a king and queen at a royal banquet, and another in which the queen launches an attempt to seduce Apollonius (PSI 151 and PMil Vogliano 260).

Now, if one considers that the extant form of the *Historia* bears in its use of certain motifs a strong resemblance to Xenophon's *Ephesiaca* and other novels of this type, then it seems very likely that the original was written in Greek. And the Apollonius of the Latin texts also takes part in a royal banquet (Chs 14–17). However, the Latin and Greek banquet scenes show no mutual similarities in their wording and there is nothing in the *Historia* that corresponds to the erotic scene in the papyrus. If the *Historia* really is based on the Greek text we have in the fragments, then it must be not only an abridged version, but also one in which considerable changes were made to the contents of the original. Perhaps the story had already been adapted in a pagan Greek or Latin text which was then used by the author of the surviving epitome; the abridgement would then be the result of efforts to Christianize this 'Apollonius Romance'. Such avenues of thought are, of course, highly speculative and do not allow us to class the *Historia* as the Latin version of a lost idealistic novel of the same type as Xenophon's *Ephesiaca*. Consequently we cannot remove the text from its place amongst the 'fringe novels'.

A definition of the genre

We are now at the end of our review of works belonging to this peripheral group. We have seen that the texts in question are akin to the idealistic and comic-realistic love-and-adventure novels in their motifs, some even very closely related. If we were to apply the modern definition of the genre 'novel', which covers a very wide spectrum of narrative prose, we would probably find it quite simple to class all these works as novels. In antiquity, however, no readers or critics are likely even to have considered counting Iambulus' 'travelogue', the *Life of Aesop*, the collected pseudepigraphic letters of Hippocrates, the *Ephemeris* of Dictys and the *Historia Apollonii regis Tyri* together with Chariton's *Callirhoe* and Petronius' *Satyrica* as variations of one and the same literary genre. The term 'ancient novel' should, therefore, only be used to refer to the idealistic novels and to those works clearly derived from them and containing constant associative links, i.e. the comic-realistic novels. These two types alone form a homogeneous group of purely fictional tales which ancient literary critics, had they actually seen their way to discussing such texts, would doubtlessly have been willing to acknowledge as a self-consistent genre.

Only these texts, then, are to be considered in our introduction to the ancient novel. To sum up the most important characteristics in a definition of the genre: by 'ancient novel' we mean an entirely fictitious story narrated in prose and ruled in its course by erotic motifs and a series of adventures which mostly take place during a journey and which can be differentiated into a number of specific, fixed patterns. The protagonists or protagonist live(s) in a realistically portrayed world which, even when set by the author in an age long since past, essentially reflects everyday life around the Mediterranean in late Hellenistic and Imperial societies; the actual characters, however, are given idealistic or comic-realistic features.

The individual works belonging to the genre are to be discussed here, as far as our limited knowledge of the authors and their dates will allow, in chronological order, tracing the development of this literary form from the first century BC to the third or fourth AD.

2

THE RISE OF THE GENRE

Theories on the origins

The first question to be considered in any discussion of the ancient novel in its historical and literary context is naturally that of its origins, the genre being something of an anomaly within the gamut of classical Greek and Latin literature. It was therefore only right and proper that Erwin Rohde, whose large-scale monograph *Der griechische Roman und seine Vorläufer* sparked off modern research into this subject some 120 years ago now, should concentrate principally on the problem of the novel's genesis. Unfortunately, scholars working on the genre tended to dwell thenceforth on this one aspect so that, until the 1960s at least, findings were limited in the main to theories on possible forerunners. Rohde cannot be entirely exempted from the blame for this. His methods were, it is true, quite typical for the age of historicism – with its focus not on the literary works in question, but on the sources to be revealed behind them. However, in the case of the novel there was one further reason for such neglect of the actual texts at the centre of the quest for forerunners: in the eyes of late nineteenth-century classical scholars ancient narrative prose had next to no aesthetic value as literature. It was this one-sided way of thinking, not the soon obsolescent historicist approach, that continued to dominate studies on the genre until some twenty-five years ago.

Considering the resemblance of the ancient novel to popular fiction of the last two centuries and to the adventure films and television serials of very recent times, it seems reasonable to assume that modern-day critics would first look into the socio-political and cultural circumstances which contributed to the rise of the genre. There was, however, a third reason for the prolonged lack of any such efforts and for the persistence still shown not so long ago in the hunt for forerunners. A combination of factors was at play here – the absence of a clearly proven first, 'founder' novel, the fragmentary nature of the oldest surviving texts, the very scanty particulars given by the authors as to their person and their literary intentions, and, as mentioned in Chapter 1, the silence of ancient literary critics on this subject. All this made it very difficult, if not impossible, to pinpoint any origins for the genre, although its beginnings actually lie comparatively late. Hence none of the numerous hypotheses put forward by Rohde and his successors could boast a basis solid enough to make them convincing and widely acceptable, and so scholars simply went on trying to solve this one problem of the genre's origins. The novel has consequently been seen to be derived from practically every available literary form that is in some way narrative: from epic, Hellenistic historiography, the novella, fantastic travel tales, love poetry, folk stories and other types of popular narrative, from drama – particularly from comedy and mime – and from school exercises in rhetoric. Some scholars have believed that the novel's forerunners are to be found outside Greece in eastern Hellenistic mythology or Egyptian prose narrative. In a recent contribution along these lines Graham Anderson is even convinced that 'a final solution is at hand' in the shape of cuneiform texts from ancient Sumer.

The novel as a product of political, social and cultural upheavals

Research on the question of origins obviously has its merits too. The parallels it has uncovered between the ancient novel and more or less all of these literary 'forerunners' are striking. However, the point raised by B. E. Perry in 1967 does seem only legitimate (and remarkable in so far as it had not occurred to anyone earlier) – namely whether the genesis of a literary form which reflects specific trends of its age and the particular demands of its intended audience really always entails a development comparable to evolutionary processes in nature, being bred, as it were, from existing genres. An examination of the view of life expressed in the new literary genus, side by side with a look at the socio-political situation at the time of its genesis, would perhaps show that certain newly created circumstances led an original author to rise to the occasion by inventing a completely new genre, or, as Perry put it: 'The first romance was deliberately planned and written by an individual author, its inventor. He conceived it on a Tuesday afternoon in July, or some other day or month of the year' (*The Ancient Romances*, p. 175). And indeed the ancient novel does give voice to a state of mind which had never before in Greece sought its outlet in narrative literature. It expresses an outlook on life which today would be labelled 'escapism'. In this too the ancient novel resembles the 'dream factory' of the modern film and television world. The novels of antiquity are principally designed to indulge the consumer's need to compensate private problems by withdrawing into a make-believe world.

The credit for being the first to note this phenomenon, at least in its basic tenor, must be given to one of those very scholars who developed the above-listed hypotheses on the novel's origins, one to boot who may without a doubt be regarded as mistaken in his ideas. I mean Reinhold Merkelbach, who attempts to interpret almost all the surviving novels of antiquity as mystery texts for the ritual cults of Isis, Dionysus, etc. There is no need for us to examine this theory in any depth, since its underlying assumptions have already been disproved several times and it is now almost unanimously rejected by scholars. None the less, one theme which plays a role in the world of mystery cults and in the ancient novel alike, and which prompted Merkelbach to write his book, remains important. Initiates who pass successfully through cult trials can expect their god to keep them from harm on earth and free them spiritually from troubles and fears, and they can look forward to eternal bliss after death. For the heroes of novels a similar fate is in store, as the example of Xenophon's *Ephesiaca* has shown us: after a chain of trials and tribulations a happy ending awaits in the eventual safe haven of a blissful marriage. What we have in both cases is a myth, an idealistic vision of man's journey through life – the one a religious, the other a profane myth of salvation. The addressee for such myths was and has at all times been the individual with his focus on private problems, on everyday worries in the family and at work. Susceptibility to the dreams evoked by religious, philosophical or narrative literature is always at its highest during periods of political, social and economic change which the individual in the state affected cannot himself influence in any way. And it is a situation such as this that we find in the Greek-speaking world of late Hellenism and early Imperial times.

Not long before the rise of the novel, a political upheaval took place in these regions, one which probably had the most far-reaching consequences possible for the forms of community life existing until then. Alexander's conquests and the division of his empire into the kingdoms of his successors robbed the Greek polis of the power it had wielded in the Classical period. The once autonomous city states had to submit to the supremacy of monarchs, and their citizens, with the exception of the wealthy few who were allowed to hold high offices in the capital, were excluded from all responsible government positions. Because the new governing body was literally a distant power for most of its subjects, there was probably a certain degree of bewilderment on the part of the average individual. He could no longer be sure whether he could still expect the state to protect his particular political and economic interests. The wars which followed this upheaval and the increasing number of organized brigands and pirates must certainly have posed a considerable threat to the private fortunes of individual citizens. After power had passed from Alexander's successors to the Romans and after the fall of the Roman Republic, with the consequent end to wars and pirate terrorism, life became on the one hand more peaceful, and the economic situation probably took a turn for the better in most cases. On the other hand, however, politics and government were now in the hands of men who, for Greek citizens, were truly alien. Individuals therefore had all the more reason to concentrate on their private lives and perhaps occasionally indulge in the kind of escapist literature which could transport them to a more attractive, fantasy world.

This re-orienting of the private individual, who was now alienated from public life and withdrew instead into his own personal sphere, is first tangibly reflected in literature of the period around the turn of the fourth to the third century BC with the flowering of

31

New Comedy in Athens. One hundred years earlier Aristophanes had caricatured political, economic and cultural conditions in the city state and had even brought leading representatives of the polis community on to the stage. Now, in the same theatre, Menander gave prominence instead to the family, and the difficulties faced by a young lover before finally being allowed to marry his girl were used to mirror the everyday cares of the average citizen. This new type of comedy was still written for the polis audience, but the plays are unmistakably influenced by an awareness of change. There appear on stage officers returning home from wars fought far afield, or occasionally relatives who have been separated by such wars or who have lost sight of one another after being shipwrecked or attacked by pirates and are now reunited. This reflects the situation of the polis as a plaything at the mercy of foreign powers. And the ancient novel takes the next, inevitable step to complete the inclusion of this world within its own: it extends the narrow confines of the polis boards into a stage covering the entire eastern Mediterranean.

The novel as 'closet drama' and 'bourgeois prose epic'

It is, then, clear that the thematic proximity of the ancient novel to New Comedy – something first observed in antiquity itself (see above, p. 8) – is not, as one of the countless theories on the origins would have it, due to genetic extraction of the narrative from the dramatic genre. Both literary forms owe their rise to the political and social status quo of an age in which consumers of literary products had a particularly intense desire to compensate in some way for circumstances which they found to be negative for them-selves. A comparison of Menander's work and the novel shows, moreover, that there is a difference not only in the actual territory covered by the fictional worlds portrayed in the two, but also in the possibilities each had for presenting their respective 'realities' to the public. The comedian was confined to the Dionysus theatre in Athens, or to other such venues, and could thus only reach urban bourgeois society. The novel's tale was offered in the form of a book, so that every inhabitant of the Greek-speaking world, even in regions without a theatre, now had access to a literary world of fantasy which reflected the reality of his own life and reconciled him to it. Here it becomes even more evident that there was no 'biological' transformation of one genre into another, but that an existing literary form was superseded by one which was similar, but had the better means of reaching out to audiences. The theatre-goer in the closed society of the polis was supplanted by the reader somewhere in any of the Hellenistic kingdoms or later Roman provinces.

The 'substitutive' role played by the novel applies not only in the case of comedy, but also in that of another literary genre which has similarly been styled the novel's 'forerunner', this time more on the basis of formal aspects and length than because of any similarity in theme – I mean epic. It too had addressed an audience embedded within a specific social structure: the closed society of Archaic nobility. And here again, the circumstances conditional to this order were no longer given in the Hellenistic period. Polished heroic verse singing of the battles and adventures of mythical heroes gave way to simple prose telling of the dangers faced by young lovers in a hostile world. The shift was not a result of 'procreation', with a new genre rising from the old. It was once again merely the natural consequence of a change in the socio-political factors which determine the production and consumption of literature.

The novel's ancient readership

It was, however, by no means the case that the existence of this new kind of 'closet drama' and 'bourgeois prose epic' offered in the shape of the novel meant that no further comedies or epics were written. There was still an audience for both in Hellenistic and Imperial society, and this brings us to the question of the novel's readership. Which were the social strata that wanted to read about their heroes not in the hitherto presented form, but in a new, alternative one? Given the similarity between the surviving novels of antiquity and modern popular literature, and given the fact that the genre is neither discussed by ancient theorists nor can be seen to have had any appreciable influence on other literature of late antiquity, we could be led into thinking that we must picture the novel's reader as someone of little learning and accordingly low social standing. We could also substantiate this assumption by pointing out that in the Hellenistic period, and even more so in Imperial times, illiteracy amongst the lower classes was considerably reduced; the production and circulation of books, moreover, had increased to such an extent that analogies may be drawn between the business then and publishing and bookselling in later centuries. However, our scant knowledge of the social structure of ancient readerships poses a serious hindrance to finding the definitive answer on this point. Only this much can be said with any degree of certainty: the number of people who were able and could afford to read a book purely for entertainment was still quite small and comprised for the most part members of the upper and middle classes.

Within this group, novels quite probably even enjoyed a certain popularity. There is no explicit evidence for this, but we have one indication from the Imperial age that would seem to corroborate the assumption. As we saw above (p. 22), the canonical *Acts of the Apostles* uses typical novel motifs, and these were later to form the framework for a large body of apocryphal *Acts*. The simplest explanation for this is probably that the authors wanted to secure from the start the greatest possible range of impact for their literary Christian propaganda. It is true that, amongst the papyri discovered so far, those which contain novel texts are clearly outnumbered by those containing works of classical-school authors; this has been interpreted as an indication of the genre's low circulation. But do statistics signify anything at all in this case? It is not inconceivable that, in terms of preservation, classical texts fared better than editions of novels, because books which were thought of as vehicles of culture and learning were kept longer than those which were primarily read for entertainment.

Whatever the case, the ancient novels could offer something for all tastes. The reader looking for entertainment alone found an exciting plot and assorted descriptions of foreign lands. This audience probably included the businessmen whose balance sheets were, as the papyri reveal, turned over and re-used for copying novel texts. Their tastes also seem to have been shared by some of the more well-to-do; we have fragments from 'de luxe' editions, and mosaics found in a villa near the ancient Syrian capital Antioch depict, as we shall see shortly, scenes from *Ninus* and *Parthenope*. The educated reader who was well versed in literature would find in almost all of the ancient novels we have today – perhaps not in Xenophon of Ephesus, but all the more so in Heliodorus, for example – scope enough for testing his ability to recognize allusions to several centuries of Greek prose and poetic works. Furthermore, the genre's readership probably also comprised one particular group whose interest in the novel may be inferred from Antonius Diogenes' dedication of *The Wonders Beyond Thule* to his sister: the female audience. Most of the surviving texts offer a strikingly large variety of opportunities for women readers to identify with the characters in the story. It is not so much the central role given to female chastity that could have touched such chords – especially since this theme is more likely to have appealed to male readers with their particular hopes and fancies. Of greater interest for women readers was probably the frequent portrayal of the heroines as more active, more intelligent and more likeable than their often almost colourless lovers.

Novel and historiography

To end this digression on the novel's readership in antiquity and return to the problem of origins, our consideration of the question ought to have shown that the genre cannot be conceived as having evolved from another, older literary form (e.g. epic). The first Greek novel must instead have been a creation moulded with full intent by an (as yet unknown) author who responded to the political, social and cultural upheavals of the Hellenistic age by providing an alternative world in the form of romantic fiction. But rejection of the evolution theory does not necessarily implicate exclusion of the possibility that the anonymous author writing on that 'Tuesday afternoon in July' chose to model the literary framework for his idea on a specific existing genre. He and his successors decided to portray their fictional realities by means of a longish prose narrative set in the past and mostly written in the third person, and this is a method clearly reminiscent of historiography, where actual facts are recounted in the same outward form. Similarity in appearance to a historical text is indeed one of the most striking characteristics of the ancient novel, and we must therefore now consider what connection there is between this aspect and the origins of the genre.

The devices of which the novelist can avail himself in order to lend his prose narrative a historiographical note begin with his choice of title. He can use an appellation of the type otherwise found in ethnographic–geographic historiography (*Aethiopica*, *Ephesiaca*, *Babyloniaca*, etc.). To this can be added the name of a famous historian as pseudonym. We are told that, in addition to the Xenophon of Ephesus who wrote the *Ephesiaca*, a Xenophon of Antioch wrote an erotic novel entitled *Babyloniaca*, and a Xenophon of Cyprus wrote the *Cypriaca*. It is hard to believe that this is in each case the author's real name. Several surviving novels are clothed at the outset in a guise of historicity, a pretence which in the case of Antonius Diogenes' *The Wonders Beyond Thule* is particularly elaborate. In the older texts, the heroes and some of the other characters involved are historical personages: the Assyrian king in *Ninus*, the Egyptian king in *Sesonchosis*; a daughter of the Syracusan general Hermocrates, and King Artaxerxes II of Persia (fifth/fourth century BC) in Chariton's *Callirhoe*; a daughter of Polycrates, tyrant of Samos, and Metiochus, son of the Athenian general Miltiades, together with the philosopher Anaximenes and the poet Ibycus (sixth/fifth century BC) in *Parthenope*, and the philosopher Pythagoras and the tyrant Aenesidemus of Leontini (*c.* 490 BC) in *The Wonders Beyond Thule*.

Figures such as these do not appear in the later novels, but even Heliodorus in his *Aethiopica* – the youngest of the surviving texts – still keeps up the pretence and poses as a historian, noting on various occasions that he 'believes' or that 'it seems' to him that this was 'perhaps' the way things happened. Sometimes he gives merely approximative details of distance or time, or even offers alternative versions of the course of events in a given episode, although as omniscient author he has no reason for doing so. And in all extant novels we find historiographical techniques of presentation imitated at every turn – in structure, division into books, diction and style, even in allusions to famous historical works. Lastly, we must mention in this context the geographical and ethnographical digressions so reminiscent of those in Herodotus. It is therefore hardly surprising that the *Suda* – a Byzantine encyclopaedia drawn from ancient sources – at one point labels several authors of ancient novels as *historikoi*. Significant too is a passage in a letter written by

Emperor Julian in 363 (p. 301 B); he advises here against reading 'made-up stories' (*plasmata*) which seem outwardly to be historical texts, but in reality contain love-stories.

The numerous parallels between the ancient novel and historiography formed the basis of a theory on the novel's origins first expounded at the beginning of this century and still supported in recent times by a few scholars. Their hypothesis is that the novel was directly descended from Hellenistic historiography. The latter had itself already tended to embellish historical reports with novel-like detail, or had even supplemented them with fictional events designed, like scenes from tragedy, to arouse fear and pity in the reader. We may not have, so the argumentation runs, any texts which represent a genealogical link between works that can still be classed as historiography and novels of the type found in the *Ninus* fragments, but in the *Alexander Romance* history and fiction stand side by side, and this shows us that there was no fixed borderline between fact and fantasy at this time. However, the ability of Hellenistic historians and novelists to differentiate between fiction and reality is by no means as doubtful as this theory would suggest – it is in fact clearly documented. We have, first, a group of narratives possibly first composed in the Hellenistic period, namely the eye-witness reports from Troy which, as we saw above (pp. 21–2), turn a fictional story into authenticated history. Playing as they do with myth and fact, the authors show indirectly that they are quite able to distinguish between the two realms. Furthermore, whether they were biographers of Alexander padding out the king's *vita* or Roman annalists down to Livy inserting legends from Rome's earliest days into their year-by-year accounts, ancient historians never regarded their reports as anything but serious historiographical writing. The addition of other ingredients meant that events of which the historians' actual knowledge was vague or scant could be presented as they might really have happened, making them at least serviceable for the writer's interpretation of the epoch in question. In contrast to this, the fragments of the oldest surviving novel – its subject being the love and adventures of the Assyrian prince Ninus – offer an account which, as a closer look will now show us, appears to be quite deliberately set entirely in the realm of fiction.

Ninus

The extant remnants of *Ninus* – its title may have been *Assyriaca* – are found in two papyri dating from the mid-first century. The novel was in all likelihood written before this, but not very long; the linguistic evidence suggests the first century BC, and we may therefore place it in the late Hellenistic period. The remains of the first papyrus, now preserved in Geneva and Berlin, consist of three fragments, one a scrap of just ten mutilated lines (P.Gen. 85) and two containing longer, fairly intact passages (PBerol 6926) which are separated by a gap in the papyrus and which modern editors designate as Fragments A and B. Fragment C, from the second of the papyri (now in Florence, PSI 1305) contains a shorter passage which clearly belongs to a later part of the novel than A and B. The papyri offer no clues as to the correct order of A and B, but since the wedding which is a matter for debate in A would seem already to have taken place in B, the findings of scholars who place A after B seem less convincing.

The central characters of the story are the 17-year-old Ninus and his 13-year-old beloved, who probably bore the same name as in the historical tradition: Semiramis. Fragment A begins just after Ninus' return from the first military expedition which he himself has led; he asks for Semiramis' hand in marriage, although the girl is under 15 years of age and therefore, according to the laws of the land, not yet old enough for wedlock. We are told all this in two scenes: in an appeal made by Ninus to the girl's mother, his strongest arguments being his glorious achievements so far and his chasteness during all this time; and in a parallel meeting between Semiramis and Ninus' mother, during which the maiden is so embarrassed and tearful that she cannot utter a single word. The surviving text breaks off with the beginning of a dialogue between the two mothers. Fragment B opens with a conversation which gaps in the text have made very difficult to follow. It is an argument between Ninus and Semiramis, apparently caused by the wife's unfounded jealousy; the scene closes at any rate with a pledge of fidelity. Shortly after this, Ninus goes off to fight the Armenians with one of his father's armies, for which the Hellenistic author enlists the help of Greek mercenaries and elephants. At the end of the fragment we have a detailed description of battle formations and the beginning of a speech made by the prince.

In Fragment C we find Ninus shipwrecked off the coast of Colchis and in despair. The remains of the text suggest that his wife has been dragged off as a prisoner of war. Another reason for assuming that the two are separated at some point in the novel is provided by one of the above-mentioned Antioch mosaics (see p. 34): it shows Ninus lying on a bed looking at a portrait of his beloved. The most important elements of what was possibly a two-part plot were, then, the first grand-scale test of Ninus' military prowess – a sort of 'Ninopaedia' – and, after his return to Semiramis, the novel proper, namely the separation of the two and a series of adventures with the couple happily reunited at the end.

Apart from the localities and the mention of specific wars, the fragments show absolutely no similarity to the more legend-like than historical account of Ninus and Semiramis given by Ctesias of Cnidus (early fourth century BC), a text which we are able to reconstruct on the basis of Diodorus, *Bibl. Hist.* 2.1–20. There Ninus is a typical Eastern ruler and Semiramis, who has been married once before, reigns supreme after his death, a blood-thirsty and dissolute queen bearing no resemblance whatsoever to the shy maiden in the novel. Here the couple may be nominally Assyrians, but they are portrayed, like the central figures of the later novels, as Greeks through and through, and their adventures, which already bear the mark of what would then become the typical pattern, are as fictional as their characters. *Ninus* – possibly the oldest Greek novel – offers us, then, no grounds for the assumption that the genre was evolved from novel-like, fanciful historical writing.

Sesonchosis

Closely akin to the tale of the Assyrian prince was, evidently, the novel *Sesonchosis*, the hero of which was also the son of a monarch in the ancient East. The figure of Sesonchosis is based on the historical king Senwosret I of Egypt, who reigned in the Twelfth Dynasty. The language of the three surviving fragments, all from Oxyrhynchus, is relatively unsophisticated and the novel was therefore possibly written at an early stage in the history of the genre –

perhaps in the late Hellenistic period, even if the oldest fragments date from much later times. The first remnant, from a third- or fourth-century papyrus codex (POx 1826), seems to talk of Sesonchosis' father and of the young prince's military training in particular, although it must be said that not one single sentence can be completely reconstructed here. The second fragment, from a third-century papyrus (POx 2466), is in better condition and tells us about a first Egyptian victory over an Arabian army led by a certain Webelis; precautions are taken against possible further attacks from the same quarter. The text breaks off in the middle of a sentence in which we learn that Sesonchosis had not taken part in the fighting himself, but had been told about it by one Thaïmus; we may take it from this that the prince's education had not yet been completed.

The third fragment was only discovered quite recently (POx 3319) and probably belongs to the same papyrus as the second. In it Sesonchosis already has several military campaigns behind him and has returned to Egypt, but fallen from his previous high position there. In a dialogue between the prince and one Pamounis we are told that, before he went off to the wars, Sesonchosis had been promised the hand of a princess whose father he had made his vassal, and that Sesonchosis is at present in this same king's land, incognito. Another scene shows us a girl named Meameris, who catches sight of Sesonchosis and is so affected by his handsome appearance – a case of the love at first sight so typical for the genre! – that she cannot eat one morsel at a banquet held later. The text ends with Meameris about to confide in the person next to her. We may assume that the girl is Sesonchosis' betrothed, who had been too young before the prince left for the wars to be able to recognize him now; his masquerade – a motif which fits well into a novel – will no doubt have led to a series of complications, despite which the couple were finally able to marry, the prince regaining his rightful position of power.

Any further reconstruction of the plot using the information about the Egyptian king given by Herodotus and Diodorus seems scarcely permissible when we consider the striking dissimilarity between the Ninus of the novel and the Ninus of historiography. This said, James O'Sullivan has shown keen perception in such lines of thought and his ideas have much in their favour; he suggests, for example, that Sesonchosis was ousted from power in Egypt by his brother and that the Arab Webelis is the vassal king. Nevertheless, there is nothing in the historical accounts that corresponds to the love-story and its probable consequences, and this is the very theme which – together with the portions we may construe as having dealt with the prince's education and his military adventures after the betrothal – forms the skeleton of the novel's plot. The story itself being, moreover, remarkably similar to that of *Ninus*, we therefore need not hesitate to assign *Sesonchosis* to the genre 'ancient novel' and accordingly look upon its contents as for the most part fiction invented by the author.

A genre is born

To return to the question posed above as to the connection between the novel's historiographical façade and the origins of the genre, our consideration of what are probably the two earliest exponents of this literary form brings us to the following conclusions. In spite of the historicity of the background and of the central characters, the actual events depicted in these novels do not represent the expansion of a historical core, as can be said, for example, of the *Alexander Romance*. They are instead entirely fictitious. The theory which postulates a gradual transition from Hellenistic historiography to the novel must therefore be rejected. This, in turn, means that the use of a pseudo-historical guise for fictional reality can be interpreted as the author's attempt to create an atmosphere of seriousness for the view of the world to be conveyed by his story. And, significantly, there is an interesting parallel to such tactics in Xenophon of Athens, whom we have just seen to be a particularly popular novelist's model. The underlying intention of the *Cyropaedia* – without a doubt the text directly imitated in the early chapters of *Ninus* and *Sesonchosis* – had to do, as we saw above (p. 15), with political philosophy: the work was to be a portrait of the ideal ruler. However, the historical Cyrus could only qualify as such after Xenophon had thought up a new *vita* for him. Presented as authentic biography, its effect on the reader was much greater than that of a patently fictitious 'life and times' would have been. And, similarly, when the type of adventures used in New Comedy to reflect prevalent social conditions were first depicted in narrative prose for the same purpose, the authors in question could also hope to arouse livelier interest in their works by giving them a historiographical façade. That their principal source of inspiration for this new literary form was indeed the *Cyropaedia* may be concluded from one further observation which has frequently been made. The historian Xenophon himself had already interwoven the fate of his central figure with a love-story, if only very loosely (see above, p. 15). Now, the first novelists made their heroes – likewise rulers over ancient Eastern kingdoms – fall in love themselves.

Summing up, we can say that the ancient novel did not evolve genetically from an existing, thematically similar genre or from one comparable in terms of narrative technique. The origins can be traced instead to the specific political, social and cultural conditions prevalent in the late Hellenistic period. As an alternative to this reality, novelists offered a fictional, idealized world. By presenting their stories with the aid of devices traditionally used by historiographers to depict the real world, they were able to underline the serious side of their new genre and thus attract readers.

3

THE IDEALISTIC NOVEL IN EARLY IMPERIAL TIMES

Chariton, *Callirhoe*

Probably the <u>earliest of the fully extant ancient novels</u>, Chariton's <u>Callirhoe</u> survives as a complete text in only one single manuscript from the Middle Ages. Fragments from three papyri written between 150 and 250 and from a sixth- or seventh-century palimpsest indicate, however, that the text remained to a degree popular at least until late antiquity. We know nothing of the author except for the few facts he tells us himself. He writes that he is the secretary of a rhetor and that he hails from Aphrodisias, a city in southwestern Asia Minor. His Greek points to a date roughly in the first half of the first century, if not in fact even earlier – to the period immediately before the birth of Christ. The probable *terminus ante quem* seems to be provided by Persius in the last line of his first satire, written by the year 62 at the latest. There, readers for whom his own work is intellectually too demanding are recommended by the poet to try 'an edict' in the morning and 'Callirhoe' after lunch. This one name alone was in all likelihood the original title of the novel, as the author's final words would at any rate seem to suggest: 'This much I wrote about Callirhoe.' The work is also cited as 'Chaereas and Callirhoe', but this title undoubtedly first came into use in the Byzantine period. Another possibility is that the novel had a pseudo-historiographical title – 'Sicelica' – because the story begins and ends in the Sicilian city of Syracuse in the fifth/fourth century BC.

As in Xenophon of Ephesus, <u>the two lovers around whom the</u> <u>story revolves marry at the beginning and are torn asunder shortly</u>

43

after the wedding. The adventures then undergone separately by Chaereas and Callirhoe are, however, not recounted in a series of short, rapidly alternating episodes as found in the *Ephesiaca*, but in longer story blocks; these provide the basis for the novel's division into eight books. In the first two books the fate of Callirhoe figures most prominently, in the third and fourth the sufferings of Chaereas; in books 5 and 6 both are actually in the same place but still kept apart, and in the last two books the emphasis lies again on Chaereas' experiences. The first four books correspond in their total length roughly to one roll of papyrus, as do the last four, and at the beginning of book 5 readers are given a brief recapitulation of the story so far. There is therefore much to be said for the theory put forward by some scholars that we have here a 'novel in instalments'. At the beginning of the last book there is even a list of the principal narrative motifs occurring within the novel. This is particularly significant because Chariton is quite clearly thinking here of the compensatory effect he wants his novel to have, a function discussed at some length in Chapter 1. He writes:

> I think that this last book in particular will be very agreeable to readers, for it brings relief from the distressing things in the earlier books. In it there will be no more robbery, no slavery, no legal proceedings, no fighting, no thought of suicide, no war, no captivity, just rightful love and lawful marriage.

Chaereas loses his wife, daughter of the general Hermocrates, after a plot devised by her rejected suitors goads him into kicking her violently; she falls down insensible and, presumed dead, is buried. Her tomb is soon looted and the robbers take her to Miletus, where she is sold as a slave to Dionysius, the city's most noble citizen; he immediately falls in love with her and wants her for his own. Being pregnant by Chaereas, Callirhoe decides to marry Dionysius for the sake of her otherwise fatherless child and its future social status. An act of desperation unique amongst the stock motifs in extant ancient novels, this still does not protect her from further amorous advances, because all who see her take her at first glance to be Aphrodite. Chaereas has meanwhile already started to search for his wife and, having been informed of her fate by the robbers' leader, soon follows her to Miletus, but is taken into slavery and falls into the hands of Mithridates, satrap in the neighbouring land of Caria. The latter has been in love with Callirhoe for some time and now tries to help Chaereas in the hope of winning the girl for himself. Dionysius suspects Mithridates of attempting to cuckold him and complains to Pharnaces, satrap of Lydia and Ionia; this Persian, however, is also in love with Callirhoe and therefore passes the matter on to the king. The first half of the novel ends with Dionysius and Mithridates being summoned for a hearing before the court. As the author mentions in passing that King Artaxerxes is also anxious to meet the girl who is so famed for her beauty, it is not hard to guess who Callirhoe's next admirer will be.

The court case now opens the second half of the novel and a whole range of techniques normally found in drama is put into operation to depict this climax. It culminates in the surprise appearance, arranged by Mithridates, of Chaereas, whom Callirhoe and Dionysius had for some time presumed dead. The question of Callirhoe's legal husband for the future remains, however, undecided. Artaxerxes reserves judgement until a later date and uses the time he has gained to let Callirhoe know – through the mouth of his confidant – that he loves her. His approaches are interrupted by a rebellion in the Persian province of Egypt, and this creates a completely new situation. Chaereas, who has so far shown little active participation in events, now has a chance to take his revenge on Artaxerxes by proving his worth as a general on the Egyptian side. Although his rival Dionysius, fighting in the Persian army, is also brilliant on the battlefield and contributes greatly to the final crushing of the rebellion, Chaereas manages to take the city of Tyre and then the island of Aradus, to which Artaxerxes had sent his harem and with it Callirhoe. The soldierly energy shown by Chaereas comes as something of a surprise, and no less than the whole of book 7 is devoted to these military activities. The depiction of the lover as a fighting hero was to be used again as a motif in Iamblichus' *Babyloniaca*, but there are otherwise no traces of it in the later novels. The motif stems ultimately from Xenophon of Athens' *Cyropaedia*, and in this case the choice of setting makes it reminiscent of the *Alexander Romance*. It would probably have been given greater prominence in earlier novels of the type represented by the *Ninus* and *Sesonchosis* fragments. To return to the plot: this section is contrasted at the end of book 7 and the beginning of book 8 by a short interlude staged like a scene from comedy. It serves to prolong the suspense and misery briefly before the couple finally recognize one another and collapse as one, overcome with the joy of being reunited. Then at last they return to Syracuse and spend the rest of their lives there in marital bliss.

In addition to the structural clarity of the plot, one particularly striking characteristic of Chariton's narrative technique is a method which the two above-mentioned scenes 'court case' and 'recognition' have illustrated briefly, namely the dramatization of lengthy stretches of the story. Calculations have shown that approximately 90 per cent of the action is presented in the form of stage-like scenes, with about half of these in direct speech. Only 10 per cent is straightforward reporting of facts. By allowing his protagonists to take the floor themselves – and this quite often in long monologues – the author partially transposes outward events into mental processes and is thus frequently able to go beyond the bounds set by the rules of the genre in psychological characterization. Particularly with his minor characters – the robbers' leader Theron, for example – he has succeeded in creating figures that show individual profile. Rohde's unfavourable remarks on Chariton's performance as a writer are therefore – as a number of perceptive studies have now shown – unwarranted. The same applies to the judgement passed on Chariton's style: schooled as it was by the works of the historian Xenophon, the simple and objective manner adopted in *Callirhoe* is scarcely done justice with attributes such as 'colourless'.

Xenophon and other historiographers quite generally had an even greater influence on Chariton's novel than on the doubtlessly earlier *Ninus* (as far as can be ascertained from the fragments). This is made manifest in the very first sentence: 'I, Chariton of Aphrodisias, secretary to the rhetor Athenagoras, am going to tell of a passionate love which befell in Syracuse.' The wording is clearly meant to be reminiscent of the traditional opening lines in earlier historical works, for example in Thucydides: 'Thucydides of Athens wrote the history of the war between the Peloponnesians and the Athenians.' Chariton's summaries of foregoing events have been compared with the brief recapitulations found in the manuscripts at the beginning of books 2–5 of Xenophon's *Anabasis*. It has also been noted that the titles *Anabasis* and *Cyropaedia* bear in each case direct reference only to the first book of the work, much in the same way as Chariton announces a love-story taking place in Syracuse, but changes the scene of events at the end of the first book. Not wishing to add unnecessarily to these instances of Chariton's imitation of the historian Xenophon, I shall draw the reader's attention to only one other point: the racy parallel between the march of the Ten Thousand against Artaxerxes II described at the beginning of the *Anabasis*, and the journey undertaken by Callirhoe's rivalling infatuates to the court of the same Persian king.

Chariton's dating of his story to Greece's Classical period, rather than to the distant past of a once grand empire, shows how closely he follows the foremost Attic historians in content too. This represents an important step in the development of the genre. Greek-speaking readers could undoubtedly feel greater affinity with Greek men and women from the fifth and fourth centuries BC, who were familiar to them from the accounts given in the manifold literary works of that age, than with the sons and daughters of Eastern rulers. And it was not to be long before readers would duly identify with the characters in the novels without the authors having to use the type of historical colouring which, in the early days of the genre, was apparently indispensable. One reason for the appeal which Chariton – and similarly the author of *Parthenope* – clearly believed Greece's Classical period would hold for their readers may have been the political situation of the age in which each of the works was probably written. Octavian's victory at Actium in 31 BC had finally put an end to the wars which, after the death of Alexander and the dissolution of his empire, had been visited again and again on the Greek inhabitants of eastern Mediterranean countries. The Augustan era was soon to bring widespread peace, and this aroused in the states which had been independent under Alexander's successors, but were now united under Roman rule, a new feeling of solidarity. It manifested itself in retrospects of the glorious past and, more especially, in the rediscovery of the language and literature of Athens. This nostalgia can also be interpreted as a form of escape from the present; thus ancient Hellas has here the function of an ideal world for escapist reading.

Chariton's romanticized account of the adventures undergone by (pseudo-)historical Greeks living in the heyday of the polis has quite rightly been termed a myth. In the 'bourgeois prose epic' of the early Imperial age, it takes the place of the myth of the noble hero in Homeric epic. This comparison between the social function of the novel and that of epic has also provided a plausible explanation for one striking device used by Chariton. At twenty-seven points in his novel he interrupts his prose narrative to quote one or several verses from the *Iliad* or from the *Odyssey*. When Chaereas, for example, announces that he wants to fight against Artaxerxes (7.2) he says:

> Considering all the adversity I have been through, I should have been dead long ago, but from now on I am going to live for the one purpose of harming my enemy.
>   Verily, let me not die without struggle and not without glory,
>   but with a feat to my name which posterity too will be told of.

These occasional borrowings from his great epic-writing predecessor clearly represent Chariton's attempt to build a bridge to another acknowledged genre. Like the historiographical guise, this second link is supposed to help ensure that the new narrative form he has chosen will be accepted and taken seriously by well-read audiences. Chariton not only quite consciously intends the contents of his novel as a sort of myth of salvation tailored to fit the political situation in his own time. He also understands his book as the form of 'epic' representation of this myth most suited to the needs of his contemporaries, and he accordingly sees himself as a kind of modern Homer.

Other novels in historical dress:
Parthenope, Chione, Calligone

While Chariton took historical material for his *Callirhoe* from Thucydides and Xenophon, the author of *Parthenope* borrowed from Herodotus, using the figures of Metiochus, son of the Athenian general Miltiades, for his young *inamorato*, and the tyrant Polycrates of Samos for the father of his heroine Parthenope. In a

48

remarkable feat of papyrological expertise, three fragments from a second-century papyrus (all in Berlin: PBerol 7927, 9588 and 21179) have been joined to reconstruct two fairly intact columns of text. They contain part of an after-dinner party at the court of Polycrates from the beginning of the novel.

The scene must have been preceded by the first meeting between the tyrant's guest, Metiochus, and Parthenope; the two had fallen in love at first sight. At the beginning of the fragment Polycrates, who is apparently ignorant of all this, declares that he could well imagine having Metiochus as son-in-law; he then invites everyone to drink and embark upon a discussion of Eros, chaired by the philosopher Anaximenes. The first to speak in the debate – it is modelled on Plato's *Symposium* – is Metiochus. His is a rational point of view, expressing doubt as to the existence of such a divine force as Eros and his weapons; he himself has never known love's sting and is not sure that he ever will. An enraged Parthenope, who wants to hold on to the traditional myth, begins her reply to this. The fragment ends here, but the surviving remains of a Persian adaptation of *Parthenope* give us some idea of what happened next. Transposing events in the eleventh-century verse romance *Vāmiq and ʿAdhrā* by the poet ʿUnṣurī, we may assume that the scene continued with the bard Ibycus playing on his lyre and singing of Parthenope's and Metiochus' beauty; someone then asked about the origins of the lyre and Metiochus told the tale of its invention by Hermes.

From antiquity we have scattered references to the plot of *Parthenope* and also the remains of a letter from Metiochus, found on a fragment of earthenware (O.Bodl. 2175); he writes here in despair to his beloved, from whom he has been separated. All these snatches of text make it seem probable that the couple, whose counterparts in the Persian romance had married shortly after the *symposium*, were soon forcibly parted. Parthenope went to Lower Italy and Persia in search of her husband, her chastity constantly being threatened along the way; the short fragment POx 435 possibly belongs to the account of her odyssey. Tomas Hägg, who used the above-mentioned Persian romance for his reconstruction of the novel, found further material for this in the legend of the martyrdom of Saint Parthenope. This text survives in one fragment of a Coptic version, which was probably based on a Greek original dating from late antiquity, and in an Arabic translation of the Coptic text. Hägg's deductions – Parthenope was abducted by the king of Persia and cleverly arranged her own apparent death in order to escape his advances – are convincing, since a comparative glance at Chariton's *Callirhoe* and other Greek romances shows such motifs to be entirely conceivable in a novel. Another suggestion as to the possible contents of the novel seems similarly reasonable: there are two mosaics from the ancient Syrian city of Antioch which show Parthenope and Metiochus, with the latter in military dress; these could represent a scene from the end of the novel, in which the two lovers are reunited after Metiochus' return from battle.

The striking similarities between *Parthenope* and Chariton's *Callirhoe* in their use of certain motifs and in their language make it seem probable that Chariton wrote both novels. Correspondences in these two areas are also found in the *Chione* fragments and in two remnants of a papyrus from the second or third century (PBerol 10535 and 21234). We may therefore assume that Chariton, unlike the other authors known to us, wrote more than one novel. Another indication that he was the author of *Chione* is the fact that the surviving fragments of this novel belong to the same sixth- or seventh-century palimpsest in which bits of *Callirhoe* were once discovered. Six leaves from this codex – four from book 8 of *Callirhoe* and two from the beginning of *Chione* – were found, but then lost again under very unfortunate circumstances – the manuscript was destroyed by fire in Hamburg harbour after being shipped from Egypt to Germany. All we have now are those passages which Ulrich Wilcken had managed to decipher between his own discovery of the fragments and their subsequent incineration. Parts of his transcription were made on board a boat sailing down the Nile at night, the light flickering the while, and the text of both novels was in any case mutilated, having been effaced to make room for a copy of a Coptic sermon. We are left, then, with only three columns of the novel *Chione*.

The picture conveyed to us by this text of the beginning of the work is accordingly vague. It may at least be considered possible that this novel too had a pseudo-historical background. In the first column mention is made either of kingship or of a queen. If this latter reading is the correct one, then there is much to be said for a suggestion made by Nicoletta Marini: the queen could have played a role similar to that of the wife of the Persian king Artaxerxes II in Chariton's *Callirhoe*. The heroine Chione probably ran into difficulties because she was in love not with the man chosen to be her bridegroom, but with another. The third column shows her talking apparently to her lover and hinting to him that she will kill herself if no other solution can be found. This, we may suppose, triggered off the usual chain of adventures, after which the couple will have been happily reunited. Attempts have been made to link the above-mentioned Berlin fragments with *Chione*, but their actual contents are unclear, and the conclusions drawn so far still seem rather speculative.

Finally, a historical background may also be assumed for *Calligone*, a novel which survives in two fragments of a calligraphic papyrus from the second century (PSI 981). The extant scene seems to take place somewhere in the Balkan regions during a war between the Sauromatae and the Scythians. Here again the style and contents are both reminiscent of Chariton's *Callirhoe*. We learn in simple, straightforward words that Calligone – no doubt the heroine of the novel – is ready to kill herself with a dagger in the tent of one Eubiotus; she berates him for trying to stop her. Since she tearfully curses the day she 'saw Erasinus while out hunting', the reason for her despair is probably a separation from her beloved or the assumption that he is dead. If our interpretation and dating of these and other fragments discussed above are correct, then we may conclude at this point that the first century AD saw the appearance of several novels of the same type as *Callirhoe*.

A string of adventures:
Xenophon of Ephesus, *Ephesiaca*

The *Ephesiaca* ('An Ephesian Story') of Xenophon of Ephesus, the contents of which were summarized in Chapter 1 (pp. 1–6), probably belongs to a later phase in the development of the genre. It dispenses entirely with historical trappings and presents instead an unabashed accumulation of adventures which, in number, exceed by far the comparable episodes in Chariton. This suggests that it had now become standard practice for novelists to dip into the stock of traditional elements. The *Ephesiaca* dates at the earliest from the end of the first century, because the office of *eirenarches* ('peace officer') mentioned in 2.13 does not seem to have been in existence before the reign of Trajan (98–117). A date of composition later than 150 is, on the other hand, unlikely, because a comparison with the novel written by Achilles Tatius in the latter half of the second century points to Xenophon as the elder of the two writers. We have already mentioned in Chapter 2 that the author of the *Ephesiaca* was possibly using a pseudonym, paying tribute to the genre's 'founder' (p. 36). Xenophon's Ephesian origins, cited otherwise only in the Byzantine encyclopedia, the *Suda*, are similarly hard to believe, because the details he gives about the place betray none of the special knowledge a local would have. The *Suda* maintains that the novelist also wrote a book entitled 'On the City of the Ephesians' and other works, but here too it would seem advisable to treat the entry with scepticism.

The same encyclopaedia states further that Xenophon's novel consisted of not five, but ten books. This, together with a whole series of arguments, has frequently been cited in attempts to show that the text of the *Ephesiaca* as we know it from the one surviving medieval manuscript is an abridged version. One of the main indications that our text is possibly an epitome is the frequent lack of motivation for a particular continuation of the plot; in 4.4, for example, no explanation is offered as to why Habrocomes suddenly transplants his search for Anthia from Egypt to Italy. Another sign would seem to be the rapid succession of events. The author reports these for the most part simply as facts, even almost in the form of minutes or, as Erwin Rohde put it: 'He is always in a hurry; like a surly art-gallery guide he drags us in bustling haste from one picture to the next, so that scarcely anywhere can we form a clear image of the fleeting figures passing before us' (*Der griechische Roman und seine Vorläufer*, p. 402). The followers of the epitome theory undoubtedly have more convincing arguments than its opponents. Reading the text even only in cursory fashion, it can plainly be seen that the framework for the narrative – that is, the events taking place before the couple are parted in the middle of book 2, and those leading to the happy ending in book 5 – is much more carefully structured than the adventures along the way. With regard to readership, however, and to the demands the novel was intended to meet, this particular problem is of no consequence. Whether the short novel we have today was actually written in this form or is the result of mechanical abridgement, it was certainly produced for readers who now looked to action-packed thrillers with as many different episodes as possible for their entertainment. The ancient novel was never closer to modern-day television serials than it is here.

Those sections of the *Ephesiaca* which are not thought to be abridged betray in any case the author's endeavour not to describe events, and certainly not to amplify them, but to string them together in the manner of a chronicler. Unlike Chariton, Xenophon makes no attempt to give his characters individual features, but simply has them carry out their allotted functions; this is most conspicuous in the minor roles. His language is in general almost primitive in its syntax, and he does not shrink from using stereotype expressions or the same connectives over and over again. When Xenophon does enter into detail, it is, significantly, at those points where his aim seems to be to outdo Chariton, not only by increasing the number of adventures, but also by adding melodramatic and sensational effects to the motifs he has borrowed from his predecessor in the genre. For example, when Callirhoe finds herself buried alive, she sheds the tears one would expect and is in fear of her life when the robbers break into her tomb (1.8 f.); Anthia, in the same situation, is only sorry that the poison she took was merely a sleeping draught, decides to starve herself to death instead and so later begs the robbers to leave her in the tomb (3.8).

Xenophon's efforts to improve upon the traditional stock of motifs in quantity and quality also make themselves felt in the unusually large part he allows the gods to play in events. In Chariton it had been essentially Tyche, the goddess of fate, at work, and only Aphrodite had played the conventional wrathful role familiar from epic. This motif was probably also used in *Parthenope*: we may conclude from Metiochus' speech against the power of Love, and from the devil's influence on events in the Coptic legend of Saint Parthenope, that the wrath of Eros was introduced to precipitate the plot. Xenophon too has Eros take umbrage and pursue the lovers in his rage, but the last mention of this is at the beginning of book 2. From here on the workings of various other deities can be seen, depending on where Habrocomes or Anthia happen to be staying at the time; Helius and Isis are particularly prominent in their support. While none of this should be interpreted as a moralizing message or 'profound religiosity' on the part of the author, we may certainly grant Xenophon that his treatment of the typical pattern of action as prescribed by the genre was also meant to be a little more than just entertainment. It was, in addition, his own personal contribution to the picture of trials and tribulations traditionally painted in the idealistic novel. By multiplying almost to infinity the dangers faced by his characters and frequently making the threat so great that only a miracle can help, he portrays the *conditio humana* as one of helpless isolation in a hostile world. The happy ending then comes as all the more of a surprise. Thus readers who identified with the protagonists of the novel would be allowed the illusion that their own personal problems might be solved in a similarly ideal fashion.

Lollianus, *Phoenicica*

The evaluation of papyrus fragments which came to light in a sensational find some twenty-five years ago has shown us that readers in early Imperial times had a choice not only of 'historical' novels of the type best known to us through Chariton's *Callirhoe*, but also of the kind of novel represented by Xenophon's *Ephesiaca*. There was, as we now know, at least one other novel which contained a string of adventures made as lurid and thrilling as possible, in which apparently no great store was set by the portrayal of characters with individual profiles, and which was written in an unsophisticated Greek with limited vocabulary and simple syntax: the *Phoenicica* ('A Phoenician Story') of Lollianus. What survives of this novel is found on papyrus fragments from the latter half of the second century (PColon inv. 3328) and on the back of a document roll from the first half of the third century (POx 1368). The *Phoenicica* was, then, probably written – like the *Ephesiaca* – in the first half of the second century. The Roman name Lollianus is not uncommon during this period, a fact which ought to be taken into consideration in attempts to establish the author's identity. Thus the novel need not necessarily be ascribed to P. Hordeonius Lollianus, sophist and professor of rhetoric in Athens in the mid-second century. In fact he seems an unlikely candidate, because the novels of the Second Sophistic, as we shall see in the final chapter of this book, differ considerably from the text of the *Phoenicica* fragments in content and in language. However, our knowledge of the novel is too incomplete for a positive identification or exclusion of this rhetor as its author.

Amongst the forty-six fragments of the Cologne papyrus there are four passages from which we learn most about the contents of the novel: two short texts from the end of book 1 and two longer sections, one of these ending a later book (the exact number of books cannot be established) and the other beginning the following book. In the last fragment of book 1 we read the account given by a young man of a night of love spent with a girl named Persis; it is for both their first experience of sexual intercourse. The subject and its very candid treatment are features which bring this and the other extant scenes from the *Phoenicica* clearly very close to the comic-realistic novel. It has even been noted that Lollianus uses several motifs for which parallels can be found in Petronius' *Satyrica* and in the *Ass Romance*. However, our fragments show no trace of comic or satirical traits, so we have no reason to number the *Phoenicica* amongst the comic-realistic novels.

The other surviving book-ending equals the erotic scene in its vividness. It describes in full detail how, in the presence of one Androtimus – probably the novel's hero – robbers slaughter a boy, roast his heart, halve it and pass the pieces around; all must then swear over its blood that they will never desert their leader(?) and never, either in prison or under torture, betray him. The following book opens with the orgiastic revels which take place after the butchery; the robbers' vomiting, uninhibited belching and farting thoroughly disgust Androtimus; they end the party by making love to their women before his very eyes. At midnight corpses are stripped of their clothing and either the bodies or the garments then thrown out of the window. The robbers leave the room after this, some of them wearing white with their faces covered in white lead, others wearing black with soot on their faces so that they will not be recognized. At the end of the fragment we are told that Androtimus is left behind as prisoner and is well-guarded; we then have the words 'goldsmith's workshop', but their context is unclear.

Albert Henrichs, the first editor of the Cologne fragments, held the part of the novel extending from the murder of the boy to the robbers' masquerade to be a true account of the course of the initiation ceremonies involved in the Dionysus–Zagreus mystery cult – confirmation, then, of Merkelbach's interpretation of most ancient novels as mystery texts (see above, p. 30). However, other scholars have compared the text with scenes from Xenophon of Ephesus and Achilles Tatius in which robbers plan or carry out ritual murders. The conclusions reached make it seem probable that what we have in all cases are variants of one of the genre's typical motifs, that of apparent death. We have every reason to suppose that the boy in the *Phoenicica* was not really sacrificed at all and that the 'victim', whom we may perhaps rather suppose to be a girl disguised as a boy, was Androtimus' beloved. A convincing 'profane' explanation has also been found for the strange disguises donned by the robbers: a strikingly similar scene in Apuleius' *Metamorphoses* (4.22) makes it seem plausible that the robbers were simply dressing up as black and white ghosts in order to escape recognition during their next raid (on the enigmatic goldsmith's workshop?) and to terrify their victims or anyone coming to the rescue. We may therefore also assume that the 'spooky' scene we have in the Oxyrhynchus fragment was proved at some later point in the novel to have been mere hocus-pocus, or that the reader knew this all along. This text tells us how a certain Glaucetes, who also plays a part in the fragments of book 1, is out riding one night when he is suddenly confronted with the ghost of a young man; the apparition requests that Glaucetes take the earthly remains of the ghost, together with those of a beautiful young girl buried with him under a plane tree, and lay them to rest a little further from the road. Glaucetes can only nod in stupefaction and the spectre vanishes.

An attempt to diversify:
Antonius Diogenes, *The Wonders Beyond Thule*

Both the *Ephesiaca* of Xenophon of Ephesus and Lollianus' *Phoenicica* would seem to belong to the same phase in the development of the idealistic novel. The historiographical garb needed to establish this type of text as a literary genre had been cast off and the novel consisted now of a miscellany of episodes strung together, the adventures themselves becoming increasingly fantastic. Having dispensed with all forms of artistic embellishment, it now laid no claims to being anything more than the simplest kind of entertainment. Lollianus' work, as we have just seen, shows some resemblance to the comic-realistic novel. This latter branch of the genre, with its satirical elements, must, by contrast, be accorded a much higher literary value, and we are now nearing the point where we ought to take a closer look at these texts. Before doing so, however, we must consider one other example of ancient prose fiction which is closely related to the idealistic novel. It is a work written most likely before rather than after the *Ephesiaca* and the *Phoenicica*, and one which was probably also of a higher literary quality. I mean the novel *Ta huper Thoulen apista* ('The Wonders Beyond Thule') of Antonius Diogenes. Here the conventional pattern of action found in the idealistic novel was diversified with elements taken from other types of prose fiction: from fantastic travel tales and from the fictional lives of philosophers. This approach to the genre was, as far as we can see, to remain a unique experiment. None the less, its influence on both the idealistic and comic-realistic novel was probably considerable.

The original text of Antonius Diogenes' quite singular novel is no longer extant and, of all the other works of Greek narrative literature which survive in fragments or synopses only, the loss of this one is perhaps the most lamentable. We are therefore particularly fortunate in having, apart from four short fragments, a summary of its contents, written by the ninth-century Patriarch of Constantinople Photius (cod. 166). When it comes to the reliability of this account, we are less fortunate: a comparison between the surviving text of Heliodorus' *Aethiopica* and the summary of its contents given by the same patriarch (cod. 73) shows that, if we were dependent solely on Photius for our knowledge of the plot, our picture of it would differ widely from the real thing. Nothing is known to us about the author of *The Wonders Beyond Thule* other than what the Latin part of his name tells us. He seems to have adopted the *nomen gentile* of the Antonii for some reason, and this will probably have been around 35 BC at the earliest, in the lifetime of the famous *triumvir* Marcus Antonius. The work displays some interest in the Pythagorean revival; this suggests a date in the first century, although the papyri (PMich Inv. Nr. 5 [?], PSI 1177, POx 3012 and P.Gen.inv. 187) are from the second and third centuries.

The formidable number of episodes mentioned by Photius alone makes it very difficult to present here a detailed picture of the plot, which was spread, like that of the Homeric epics, over twenty-four books. A discussion of the surviving text fragments seems even less feasible, and the complicated structural technique of the whole – 'story within a story within a story' and so forth – is not conducive to the creation even of just a satisfactory general impression, given the short space to which we are restricted here.

The section of the novel which followed roughly the pattern traditionally used in the idealistic novel was embedded in a fourfold framework and covered books 2–23. Here Dercyllis, a young woman from Tyre, told her lover Dinias how she and her brother Mantinias had been forced to flee from their native city because they had been tricked by the evil Egyptian priest and sorcerer Paapis into giving their parents a potion which would, they thought, cure them, but which in fact put them into a death-like coma. The siblings wandered through the eastern and western Mediterranean lands and their experiences there were partly adventures quite similar to those familiar from the novels centred around a young couple in love; the pair are, for example, parted at one point. Other occurrences were of a more fantastic nature, some even encounters of the 'third kind'. They ended up for a while in the far north on the island of Thule, where Paapis, who had been in pursuit all the time, cast a spell on them, leaving them in a vampire-like condition. During the day they had to lie in lifeless repose, so that Dercyllis' account was spread over a number of nights (probably twenty-two, corresponding to the number of books devoted in the novel to her narrative). Dinias, her audience for all this, had himself come to Thule in the course of a long journey in quest of knowledge. The brother and sister having been freed from the deadly spell – how this came about was related by Dinias' friend Azoulis – the explorer took up his travels again in book 24. These led him very close to the moon, and he finally returned to Tyre; Dercyllis and her brother had already arrived there too, so the three were happily reunited.

The Dinias story framing Dercyllis' narrative was itself also embedded within a nest of tales, before the start of which the author placed, in addition, a proem in the form of a letter to one Faustinus. This was followed by a dedicatory epistle to the author's sister Isidora, which in turn contained a letter in which Balagrus, body-guard to Alexander the Great, told his wife Phila how, after taking Tyre (332 BC), the king had found a box in Dinias' tomb; it contained tablets of cypress wood inscribed with the dead man's life-story. This had been put in writing by the Athenian Erasinides and was based on the account given by Dinias to a fellow-countryman, Cymbas, in Tyre; the latter had wanted to take Dinias back to his native home in Arcadia.

The stratification of the novel was not limited to this fourfold packaging of Dercyllis' adventure story and to Azoulis' account in book 24. In addition to all this Dercyllis – after the separation from her brother – met the Pythagorean Astraeus, who told her about his childhood, about that of Zamolxis (one of Pythagoras' followers who later put in an appearance personally), and about the life of the philosopher himself. Naturally Mantinias too had much to tell his sister on seeing her again; he had undergone a number of adventures, most of them very weird.

We do not know how much space was devoted within the novel to the Astraeus–Zamolxis sections, but Photius' summary suggests that they were spread over two narrative units grouped around the core of Dercyllis' account. They therefore quite probably formed the innermost ring of the entire plot. In addition to numerous miraculous tales, which were in part similar to those found in Philostratus' *Life of Apollonius of Tyana*, these two sections contained a great deal of philosophical and religious instruction; the siblings even took a trip to the underworld before they were parted. These elements have been construed as grounds for the assumption that the novel-like parts of the work merely provided the skeleton plot for a tendentious, Neopythagorean treatise. However, this theory has quite rightly been rejected, the argument against it being that the patriarch Photius, who was particularly interested in philosophical and religious themes, devotes much less space to the Astraeus section than to the mixed bag of adventures undergone by the siblings and to the fantastic experiences had by Dinias and Mantinias on their respective travels. Nowhere, furthermore, can these stories be seen to have any significance in terms of Pythagorean thought and life-style. Within the convolutions of this narrative, then, the three chief elements – taken from the idealistic novel, from fantastic travel tales and from the fictional lives of philosophers, and accordingly heterogeneous – were given equal weight and together served one purpose: the basic theme which traditionally underlay the idealistic novel – that is, that of man's wanderings through life – was to be presented this time on three different planes.

The Wonders Beyond Thule had an unmistakable influence on the later ancient novels. However, the attempt made here by Antonius Diogenes to expand the stereotype adventures described in idealistic novels by sending his characters off to fantastic regions and confronting them with philosophy and religion was, in itself, to remain an isolated venture. Leaving aside for a moment Apuleius' *Metamorphoses* and the finale in Heliodorus' *Aethiopica*, we find no authors continuing directly along these lines. The reason for this was perhaps that in their idealistic presentation of adventures undergone by ordinary men and women, the late second- and third-century successors of the earliest Hellenistic novelists still chose not to lose sight of reality.

4

THE COMIC-REALISTIC
NOVEL

Those familiar with the history of the modern European novel
will know that one of the factors which essentially determined its
development was, through into the nineteenth century, the critical
treatment given in the realistic novel to the idealized world presented in medieval and baroque romances of chivalry and heroic-
gallant tales. The clash is tangible as early as the sixteenth century
with the birth of the picaresque novel and its new type of anti-hero,
and is particularly evident in the first great novel of modern
European literature, Cervantes' *Don Quixote*: in this, chivalric
ideals are confronted with the harsh realities of life. Another author,
one who can similarly be said to belong to the vanguard of the
modern European novel, found his way to realistic representation in
the course of a composition which was intended at the outset as a
parody on the idealistic novel; the contrasting world created for this
purpose then gradually became itself the focus of the writer's
interest. Henry Fielding's *Joseph Andrews* (1742) begins as a parody
of the idealistic virtue and morality propagated in Samuel
Richardson's *Pamela*, but adheres as the story progresses more and
more to the motto stated in the preface: the work being of a new
kind, a 'comic epic-poem in prose', it must present not an ideal
('unreal') world, but one 'true to nature'.

In classical studies it has still not been fully appreciated that a
very similar process can be observed in the development of the
ancient novel. In the surviving sections of his *Satyrica*, Petronius
clearly parodies the pattern of events traditionally used in the Greek
idealistic novel, and at those points where he targets specific scenes
typical for that kind of narrative, his rendering is more caricature

61

than realism. For example: during a storm at sea the hero prays to Poseidon that he and his beloved be engulfed by one and the same wave, or that their grave be the belly of one and the same fish, as we read in Achilles Tatius' version of the motif; in the *Satyrica* we find a similar scene where the boy Giton slips under the cloak of his lover Encolpius and buckles his belt around the both of them to ensure 'that no envious wave should pull us apart as we clung to each other' (114.10). At the same time, however, there are passages in Petronius' work – most especially in the famous 'Trimalchio's Feast' – that are depicted with a blunt realism unparalleled in Roman literature. Parody of the idealistic novel and realistic narrative can also be found side by side in the Greek *Ass Romance* and, even more so, in its Latin adaptation, the *Metamorphoses* of Apuleius.

A Greek comic-realistic novel in prose and verse: *Iolaus*

Some classical scholars tend to attach little significance to Petronius' connections with the Greek novel, or even to deny that he has anything to do with the tradition. One of the main reasons for this is that the prose text of the *Satyrica* is interspersed with passages in verse, some longer, some shorter, some composed by the author himself, some quoted from other writers. This form – the *prosimetrum* – is not used in the two other extant comic-realistic novels. It is frequently traced back by scholars to a Roman prototype, to a collection of satires by M. Terentius Varro (116–27 BC): the *Saturae Menippeae*. Because satire is a genre created by the Romans and because the title of Petronius' work as transmitted in the manuscripts – *Satyrica* – seems to point in this direction, his text is defined by many as a Menippean satire. Petronius is, moreover, generally thought to have been a contemporary of the philosopher Seneca (*c.* 4–65), who himself composed a satire on the Emperor Claudius, the *Apocolocyntosis* ('Pumpkinification'), in the form of a *prosimetrum*. This provides welcome support for such a classification in Petronius' case. Until quite recently the only argument that could be brought forward against the theory was that one essential element of Roman satire – the taking of an explicit stance on a moral-philosophical question – is missing in the *Satyrica*. The hypothesis that Petronius' work must be seen as a novel connected in some way to a Greek tradition could previously only be based on the assumption that there had been a Greek parallel to the comic-realistic novel in 'prosimetrical' form; no definite proof could be presented. However, we now know that one such parallel apparently did exist. The evidence was produced in 1971 with the sensational discovery of a fragment of the novel *Iolaus*.

The surviving piece of text is in a second-century papyrus (POx 3010) and talks – at first in prose – of some unnamed person who has just been initiated into the cult of Cybele (a goddess of fertility in Asia Minor whose priests, the *Galloi*, were eunuchs). We then find this person, filled with his new mystery learning, addressing someone called Iolaus, whom he seems to want to initiate into the cult too (the text is unfortunately rather mutilated at this point). His speech consists of twenty sotadeans, a metre also used in the *Satyrica*. There follows another sentence in prose telling us that the initiate passes his knowledge of the mysteries on to Iolaus, and the fragment then ends with verses from Euripides on the value of a true friend. The language of the sotadeans is quite vulgar and they mention various adventures undergone by Iolaus, for example with an effeminate homosexual. At one point we have a reference to a sexual escapade in the words 'to cunningly lay'. The following very plausible explanation has been suggested for all this: Iolaus, like Encolpius in the *Satyrica*, was a picaresque anti-hero who disguised himself as a eunuch priest of Cybele in the hope that he would thus be able to approach a certain maiden more easily; in order to act the part more convincingly, he had his crony gain the necessary insight into the cult and pass it on to him. Whatever the case, the surviving fragment offers us the evidence lacking in former times: that there really was a Greek tradition of comic-realistic narrative combining prose with verse. And it seems reasonable to assume that this tradition was older than Petronius' *Satyrica*.

Topsy-turvy world: Petronius, *Satyrica*

It must now also be regarded as established beyond a doubt that the enigmatic title 'Satiricon' is the Greek genitive plural *saturikon* of *saturika*, with the word *liber* ('book') to be supplied here (cf. Virgil's *Georgicon liber* = *Georgica*). We are to understand it as a play on the type of title frequently used for Greek novels – *Ephesiaca*, *Phoenicica*, etc. By calling his work 'A Story from the Land of the Satyrs', Petronius makes it quite clear that his novel does not take place in the idealized world of a far-off country. His characters are drawn instead partly in the comical-satirical mode, partly with realistic features. This is signalled to us in the word 'Satyrs'. Dionysus' unrestrained and lewd companions are familiar above all from the fourth part of Greek tragic tetralogies. There, in the satyr-play, the heroic world of tragedy is parodied and ridiculed in often very coarse language. If we consider Petronius' *Satyrica* in the context of the idealistic novel, the arguments for its classification as a Menippean satire no longer seem cogent, particularly when we call to mind the verses inserted into a novel which was probably already in existence, *Callirhoe*. The Homeric hexameters there, we may assume, were meant to underline Chariton's view of himself as an author of 'epic in prose' (see above, p. 48), and this pose, in a certain sense one of heroic pathos, was also a target for ridicule in the comic-realistic novel; the sotadeans in *Iolaus*, some of them quite obscene, corroborate this assumption. And, finally, another very clear emulative echo of epic in the idealistic novel also finds its comic-realistic parallel in the *Satyrica*. While in the idealistic novel the wrath of the gods is visited on the protagonists by Aphrodite and Eros – as in the novels of Chariton and Xenophon of Ephesus, and probably also in *Parthenope* – Petronius' Encolpius offends Priapus, the god of fertility represented on statues with a disproportionately large phallus. One of his punishments is a plight never suffered by the heroes of idealistic love-stories, but one all the more commonly experienced in sexual reality: impotence (128 ff.).

Like the *Thule* novel of Antonius Diogenes, the *Satyrica* – if the author ever finished it – was probably divided into twenty-four books, in imitation of the Homeric epics. We know the surviving texts to be from books 14–16 and probably also 17–20. Unfortunately we cannot be sure where these books began and ended (modern editors therefore divide the text into chapters only), because what survives of the work has been transmitted merely in the form of excerpts. These were taken from a complete manuscript of at least the above-mentioned books, a copy which we know still existed at the end of the ninth century. The longest of these extracts, the *Cena Trimalchionis*, probably corresponds roughly in length to the text in the now lost manuscript, and it is generally thought to be a fairly faithful rendering of the original wording. The excerpts from books 14 on, before and after the *Cena*, on the other hand, frequently contain gaps of indeterminate length, and the text seems at times less than reliable. However, the available material does convey a reasonably satisfactory picture of the contents of books 14–20(?) and allows us to draw conclusions as to the central theme of the novel as a whole. We may assume, then, that the original work, like the fully extant idealistic novels known to us, told the story of two lovers and their adventures – the young, good-looking Encolpius and his beloved, a boy named Giton – but the tale was this time one of lowlife circles in the Mediterranean world. The surviving excerpts take place in an unnamed town on the coast of Campania and in Croton, which also lay in southern Italy. From some thirty short fragments handed down in the form of quotations from the novel in the works of various other authors, we learn that the two heroes were at some point also in Massilia (Marseille).

The first extant scene before the *Cena Trimalchionis* already shows us the lover Encolpius facing difficulties not unlike the sufferings of the husband/lover hero in the idealistic novel. After entering a school of rhetoric, where he listens to a public declamation and afterwards has a discussion with the rhetorician Agamemnon on the general decline of eloquence, Encolpius returns – rather late, because he loses his way – to his lodgings in the town; there he finds that his companion Ascyltus has cast his eye on Giton and has already tried to rape him. Given the circumstances, the two now rivalling friends cannot possibly stay together, but before they part, they and Giton undergo three adventures together: a quarrel (not always easy to understand as the background information is missing) with a yokel and his wife in the market-place, in the course of which the friends regain possession of a previously lost mantle with gold coins sewn into it; a nightly orgy in honour of Priapus at the house of Quartilla, with a series of obscene episodes (the gaps left by medieval excerptors are particularly noticeable here); and finally, the dinner-party at the house of the wealthy Trimalchio.

The *Cena Trimalchionis* – one of the outstanding literary creations of antiquity – could be said to represent a motif which, as the fragmentary banquet scene from *Parthenope* has shown us (see above, p. 49), was also used in the idealistic novel. However, it stands more firmly in a much older tradition for which Plato created the prototype: the philosophical *symposium*, a form of mimetic dialogue in which the participants entertain themselves with conversations on various themes and with story-telling, rather than having musicians and dancers perform before them. The wining and dining in this kind of work simply provide the occasion and the background for philosophical teachings to be presented to the reader in the shape of discussions between the host and his guests. The novelist Petronius, by contrast, gives equal weight to both elements – the succession of courses and drinks on the one hand, and the speeches and dialogues on the other. He uses them to draw a satirical picture of the way of life and thought in one particular section of Roman society: that of the freedmen who had acquired wealth and influence. Trimalchio is a parvenu, his profile part caricature, part realistic portrayal. He flaunts his wealth by offering new culinary delicacies, each one more extravagant than the last; he insists on airing his smattering of knowledge in grotesque discussions of astrology, medicine, rhetoric, mythology, art and literature; and he thinks nothing of giving his guests a ringside view of his private life, letting them see how he and his favourite boy fondle one another or how he quarrels violently with his wife. The tasteless vulgarities culminate in the reading of his will and a rehearsal for his own funeral. Between Trimalchio's performances we have conversations held by the other freedmen present, about their daily problems at work, the cost of living and their children, etc. Here, as in all Trimalchio's spouting off, Petronius has no qualms about letting these characters converse in undisguised Vulgar Latin, written down almost exactly as it was spoken in early Imperial times.

After the *Cena*, the plot continues with the temporary parting of Encolpius and Giton; a fight between Encolpius and his rival ends in the boy's surprise decision to leave his erstwhile lover and go off with Ascyltus. Before being reunited with Giton, Encolpius makes a new acquaintance in an art gallery: Eumolpus, an ageing poet down on his luck. He tells Encolpius of his earlier love for a youth in Pergamum, gives him a lecture on learning and the fine arts and, in front of a picture showing the fall of Troy, describes the painting in sixty-five iambic *senarii*, the most frequently used dialogue metre in Roman drama. Giton returns with Ascyltus, who soon disappears from the plot. The boy arouses the new friend's interest, whereupon Encolpius tries to commit suicide. The new threesome nevertheless stay together and board a ship. Only when they are out at sea does Encolpius realize that the ship's master Lichas and his passenger Tryphaena are old enemies of his. Inevitably they meet, recognize one another and fight, but are soon reconciled. Eumolpus tells everyone a story: 'The Widow of Ephesus'. This was a woman renowned far and wide for her virtue who, after the death of her husband, decided to spend the rest of her life in the vault beside his corpse. In spite of all her resolutions, she finally succumbed there to a soldier-seducer. He had been posted there to stand guard at some crosses near the vault, in order to prevent relatives of the crucified criminals from burying their dead. During one of his nightly visits to the vault, a body was taken down from a cross. The widow offered to replace it with that of her dead husband.

Storm and shipwreck then separate the newly reconciled parties. Travelling on to Croton, Eumolpus recites for his companions, Encolpius and Giton, an epic he has just composed – 295 hexameters on the civil war between Caesar and Pompey. Once in Croton, a town inhabited by such as have legacies to leave and such as live by legacy-hunting, Eumolpus passes himself off as the childless, ailing owner of a vast fortune in Africa and consequently enjoys great popularity. Encolpius becomes amorously involved with a lady named Circe, but the affair ends abruptly when he is suddenly stricken with impotence. There then follow two sequences in which an old hag, the priestess Oenothea, tries to cure Encolpius with all kinds of hocus-pocus, and Eumolpus announces that anyone wishing to inherit his money must first eat his dead flesh; the fragment breaks off here.

Even this brief summary ought to have made it sufficiently clear that Petronius uses quite a number of motifs from the idealistic novel in the composition of his plot. As we have already seen in the shipwreck scene, these themes are parodied and twisted by the Latin author. Two further examples will illustrate the point again. First, attempted suicide and apparent death: Eumolpus having lured Giton away, Encolpius decides to hang himself, but is hindered from doing so at the last minute when Giton and Eumolpus burst into the room; the boy screams and punches at Encolpius, snatches a razor from Eumolpus' servant, puts it to his throat and drops to the floor. Encolpius, overcome with grief, wants to kill himself with the same razor, but realizes that Giton is in fact unharmed: the blade was blunt, a dummy for the use of barber's apprentices (94). Second, recognition: on board ship Lichas is able to identify the man he had once loved and now hates – this being Encolpius, who is so afraid of Lichas that he has disguised himself as a slave and had his head shaved – not by the scar or mole usually spotted in ancient scenes of recognition. The tell-tale sign here is Encolpius' penis (105).

It is easily seen that these episodes ridicule the heroic pathos of scenes from the typical idealistic novel by taking it to extremes or confronting it with the hard facts of real, everyday life and thereby revealing its hollowness. It is, however, all the more difficult to discern whether Petronius does this simply to make fun of the genre targeted and amuse his readers, or whether his treatment of the motifs is the vehicle for a particular view of the world. Attempts to answer this question are further complicated by the fact that the whole story is told from the point of view of Encolpius, that is, by a first-person narrator, so that the author never addresses his readers directly. In order to uncover the intention behind Petronius' chosen presentation of fictional reality, it would then seem to be vital that we take a look at the author himself and the age in which he wrote.

In the *Annals* of the historian Tacitus mention is made (16.17,1; 18–20,1) of one Titus(?) Petronius who had been governor in Bithynia and consul, and who went on to join the inner circle of favourites at the Emperor Nero's court, becoming its *arbiter elegantiae* or 'arbiter of taste'. He was particularly suitable for this position, we are told, because he had perfected the art of leading a life devoted primarily to pleasure, not as a wastrel but with 'cultivated extravagance' (*erudito luxu*). The man's actions and words 'had a freedom and a stamp of self-abandonment which rendered them doubly acceptable by an air of native simplicity'. In the end, however, a begrudging adversary managed to ensure that Petronius fell into disgrace at court. He committed suicide in the year 66 by cutting his wrists. The dying man remained true to form, however, and had his veins bound up to prolong the process and give him time to listen not to philosophizing on the immortality of the soul, but to light-hearted songs and agreeable verses. He then dined and dozed, letting death come to him in his sleep. To Nero he left a record of the emperor's own sexual debauches, naming in each case the boys and women involved.

Careful analysis of the *Satyrica* has shown that the references to historical personages and to certain social and economic circumstances, as well as the text's close similarity in language to inscriptions and literary documents of the mid-first century, all point to a date of composition during the reign of Nero. Scholars today therefore almost unanimously regard Tacitus' Petronius as the author of the novel. An element of doubt remains, however, and indeed scepticism seems altogether appropriate when, in spite of the fact that the *Satyrica* is not actually mentioned at all in the *Annals*, not only the dating, but also the whole interpretation of the work is based on Tacitus' account of the man Petronius. This has been the path taken by a group of mostly American classicists, according to whom the *Satyrica* was written especially and exclusively for Nero and his circle of intimates; the court set, cultivated in its literary tastes but corrupt in its morals, would amuse itself together with Petronius, laughing at the hidden references, at the frivolities in the adventures of Encolpius and his fellow-rogues, and at the vulgarity of the world in which these characters moved. The novel was, it is then assumed, written purely for the entertainment of an audience with cultivated literary tastes and a refined palate. The argument is quite obviously circular: a man who led the life of a courtier under Nero is the most likely candidate for the authorship of a work full of obscenities, and the work, in turn, having almost certainly been composed during Nero's reign, can only have been written by the pleasure-seeking Petronius described in Tacitus' *Annals*.

An interpretation of the *Satyrica* in the light of its constant allusions to the idealistic novel and to the portrayal of man found there would seem to bring us on to firmer ground. These connotations definitely point to a date of composition in early Imperial times, when most of the Greek novels were written. They signal, furthermore, that the anti-hero Encolpius and his experiences in the world are to be interpreted as a deliberate contrast to the heroic lover and his sufferings. In Chariton and Xenophon of Ephesus, for example, we have the profane myth of salvation. They present to their readers noble men and women who are endowed with the best of physical and mental qualities and who pass through the greatest of dangers not only always unharmed, but also without forfeiting their chastity. This is the foil for Petronius' contrasting world, in which the lofty pathos of the ideal world is shown to be ridiculous and incompatible with reality. The cheerful message put across in the idealistic novel comes under serious attack in Petronius' work, and that this, rather than just a harmless poke at the motifs of the genre, was in fact his underlying intention is best demonstrated by a closer look at some of the detail in his 'counterwork'. The Fortuna we have here is not like the Tyche of the idealistic novel, who guarantees a happy ending. In Petronius she is a deity hostile to mankind, regularly causing things that seem to be going smoothly to take a turn for the worse; this applies, for example, to all Encolpius' amorous adventures. In the extant text, death is omni-present, be it as an actual occurrence, be it in the words and thoughts of the characters, or be it simply in allusions. A closer examination of numerous passages in the *Cena Trimalchionis*, for instance, shows that the scene of the feast – the house of a man of great wealth (Gr. *ploutos*) – symbolizes the realm of Pluto. Thus the evening Encolpius spends visiting Trimalchio stands for the descent into the underworld undertaken by epic heroes such as Odysseus or Aeneas.

It has been said that Petronius' novel is essentially one long appeal to the reader that he 'enjoy life'. Trimalchio, for example, calls upon his guests to do just this, after offering them a vintage wine and having a skeleton of silver with movable joints brought out to jiggle about for them as a sort of 'memento mori' (34). However, his *ergo vivamus* ('so let us live') is only on the face of it an echo of the unfearing Epicurean's attitude to death and of Horace's *carpe diem* ('seize the day'). *Vivere* for Trimalchio and the other freedmen means nothing more than purely materialistic striving for more and more possessions and gluttonous consump-tion of choicest foods and drinks – not the calm and temperate life recommended by Epicurus as an alternative to fear of death. Furthermore, the *Cena* progressively turns into something like a wake for Trimalchio, who ends the feast with a practice run for his own funeral. Is this really 'enjoying life'? The maidservant in the 'Widow of Ephesus' also entreats her mistress to 'live' (*vivere*: 111.12), with the result that the widow sleeps with the soldier; all this takes place, however, in the vault of a tomb, her dead husband's tomb to boot! The urge to live life to the full may be one of the dominant themes in the *Satyrica*, but we are shown again and again that those who give themselves over unrestrainedly to this urge for what they think is living are unable to differentiate between appearances and reality.

If we are looking for a reasonably reliable indication that the *Satyrica* was written during Nero's reign, then we quite possibly have one in Petronius' allusions to the epic and tragic poetry of his age. One of the two longish verse recitations made by Eumolpus, the 'Bellum civile' (119–24), was probably conceived as a contrast to the *Pharsalia* of Lucan, who died in the year 65. We may infer that Petronius was addressing a contemporary audience here. This also applies to the 'Troiae Halosis' (89) which, as its numerous stylistic echoes suggest, was meant to remind readers of messengers' accounts in the tragedies of Seneca. The intention behind Petronius' insertion of these long verse passages into his prose text has been the subject – particularly in the case of the 'Bellum civile' – of an abundance of hypotheses. These range from the assumption that he wanted to parody Lucan, to the equally vociferously maintained theory that his version was supposed to outdo that of his predecessor. It has now recently been pointed out that Eumolpus appears as the author both of the inserted verses and of the prose tales about the youth of Pergamum (85–7) and the 'Widow of Ephesus' (111 f.). His poetic flights, especially the 'Bellum civile', tend to overdo the bombastic language and the often grotesque descriptions to the point of ridicule; the 'Troiae Halosis' even earns its poet and deliverer a shower of stones from some listeners. The novellas, on the other hand, both display in style and structure a mastery rare in the narrative prose of world literature, and the tale of the widow leaves most of its audience in the novel in good humour. It is therefore quite feasible that Petronius was using the insertions to express indirectly his preference for the genre he had chosen over traditional literary forms.

Narrative prose fiction pretending to a higher literary status than epic or tragedy, *joie de vivre* with the grave in sight, a womanizer who can never quite finish the course – the *Satyrica* offers in all a 'topsy-turvy world'. The picture presented here of the life led by Encolpius and company is, then, a caricature. And so, like all literary works containing a *monde à l'envers*, Petronius' novel is, by implication, a satire on human life. Nowhere in his portrayal of the *theatrum mundi* does the author actually say that it is the vehicle for his satirical criticism of society or morals. Nevertheless, the hermeneutic signals which indicate that this work is meant to be more than just amusing entertainment are clear for all to see. The answer to the vexed question 'Petronius – artist or moralist?' would therefore be: 'both'.

Appearances and reality: the Greek *Ass Romance*

The problems posed by Petronius' work are in many respects similar to those involved in interpretations of the *Ass Romance*. They begin with the very form of presentation. The story – Lucius, a young Thessalian traveller curious to see something of the magic arts, is promptly turned into an ass and subjected as such to various adventures before regaining his human form – is likewise told not by the author, but by the hero himself. Thus the underlying intention of the work is here too very difficult to determine. The tale survives in a short Greek version and a longer Latin one: in *Loukios e Onos* ('Lucius or The Ass'), found in the manuscripts amongst the works of Lucian and having roughly the same length as a dialogue of the satirist; and in the *Metamorphoses* of Apuleius of Madaurus. The Latin version, which is divided into eleven books, is extended to include numerous short stories – for example the tale of Cupid and Psyche, a novella covering two books – whilst the *Onos* contains no such insertions. On the other hand, the adventures of the Greek Lucius correspond quite exactly to those of the Latin one, with the exception of a few short passages not found in the Greek version; even the actual wording is in some places very similar. One striking difference between the two texts is the way in which they end after the hero has been turned back into a man. The Greek author says a few words about curiosity and its price and sends Lucius back to the bosom of his family. Apuleius follows up Lucius' release from the spell with the delivered youth's transformation into a devotee of Isis and Osiris, his initiation into the mystery cult being described in some detail.

A fuller Greek version, the *Metamorphoseis* – allegedly written by the otherwise unknown Lucius of Patrae – is accessible to us only in Photius' summary of its contents (cod. 129). The patriarch compares the now lost work with the shorter *Onos* and concludes that the two versions are somehow related. His often rather obscure remarks on the plot, the division into books, the style of the lost *Metamorphoseis* and the approach taken by each author to the subject-matter have had classical scholars regularly racking their brains for over 200 years. Today, however, the vast majority are agreed as to the relationship between the two Greek versions and their connection with the *Metamorphoses* of Apuleius. The lost Greek text is now supposed to have told, probably in two books, the same story as both the surviving *Loukios e Onos* and the Latin *Metamorphoses*, and it was used by Apuleius for his adaptation of the tale. The *Onos* is quite clearly a mechanically abridged version of the *Metamorphoseis* and corresponds almost word for word to the relevant sections of the longer text, except for slight changes made before and after omissions.

It is also almost unanimously agreed that the ending of the *Metamorphoseis* was the same as that of the *Onos*, and that the Isis book at the end of the Latin text is therefore an addition made by Apuleius himself. However, opinion still differs as to whether the original version was also interspersed with short stories or not. Careful analysis of the abridged text has uncovered rifts at those points where sections which were of no importance for the epitomist's purposes were apparently omitted and little or nothing was done to bridge the resulting gap. We can therefore assume with a certain degree of probability that some of the short stories inserted by Apuleius into his plot were already included in the Greek text used by him. Others must be attributed to the Latin author himself, as undoubtedly in the case of 'Cupid and Psyche'. We would be well advised not to suppose that the number of these inserted tales was very high in the original, or that they were particularly long. It also seems likely that most of them were in the part of the narrative prior to the metamorphosis, as we have good reason to believe that the epitomist – who gave his abridged version the title *Onos* ('Ass') – left the ass sections essentially unchanged. The *Onos* accordingly forms the basis of the following summary of contents for the complete Greek version, which will hereafter be referred to as the *Ass Romance*. Where passages from the original seem to have been omitted and thus lost, the suggestions made as to the possible course of events can obviously only be of a tentative nature.

At the beginning of the story Lucius travels to Hypata and stays there as guest in the house of a notorious skinflint, Hipparchus; the host's wife is secretly a practising witch. Lucius himself is fascinated by the supernatural (*paradoxa*) and accordingly burns with curiosity. He and the maid Palaestra spend several nights together making love – the first is described at some length – and she arranges for Lucius to be a hidden observer while her mistress is in action. He sees the witch turning herself into an owl and flying away; he wants to try this out himself, but uses the wrong magic lotion. Thus the hero finds himself with the body of an ass, his thoughts and feelings, however, remaining those of a man. In the unabridged version this metamorphosis was probably preceded by a number of scenes in which Lucius listened to tales of black magic and sorcery, and had his first taste of spellcraft, for the moment an experience with no lasting effects: at night in front of Hipparchus' house three figures rushed at him in the dark and Lucius, believing them to be robbers, ran his sword through them a few times; in daylight the assailants proved to be wineskins, brought to life for a while through the magic skills of a sorceress (cf. Apuleius, *Met.* 2.32–3.18). After his metamorphosis, Lucius is taken away as a beast of burden by robbers who break into Hipparchus' house; they take him to their camp where, in the original, he will no doubt have had to listen to a series of accounts given by the men of their hazardous forays (cf. Apuleius, *Met.* 4.7–27).

The bandits' camp is the first stage of Lucius' long and harrowing journey through Thessaly and Macedon under varying ownership. His masters all wrongly believe that it is really an ass they have before them and accordingly mishandle him in every way conceivable, threaten to kill or castrate him, or tease and torment him. They also bare in his presence the true characters they normally conceal from other men. Lucius has no choice but to endure all this, because his attempts to obtain roses – the consumption of which is the only thing that will break the spell – fail. After the bandit scenes we meet, in succession, the wife and son of a herdsman on a stud farm, a group of mendicant priests of the Syrian Goddess, a baker, a market-gardener, a Roman soldier and a rich man in Thessalonica. This last master represents the final stage of Lucius' long odyssey; the man is told by his servants that the supposed ass can behave like a human and so he has Lucius perform all manner of 'tricks' for the entertainment of his guests. The panorama of different professions, social spheres and characters presented in these adventures bears unmistakably realistic features. It thus provides a Greek pendant to the description given by Petronius of the people encountered by his first-person narrator in southern Italy.

As a parallel to the erotic adventures before his transformation into an ass, Lucius has another sexual escapade before regaining his human shape. A rich lady, who had seen his performance in the house of the Thessalonian, hires him for two nights of lust. His master decides thereupon to have him publicly mount a condemned woman in the theatre, but, before the show starts, Lucius finally manages to eat some roses. He instantly turns back into a man and explains to the astonished governor in the audience that he is Lucius of Patrae, a writer of stories. The governor happens to know Lucius' family and allows him to leave for home. Before boarding ship, Lucius has one more encounter with the rich lady, a scene which is significant for our interpretation of the novel and which we shall consider more closely below.

This brief synopsis of the contents of the *Ass Romance* ought to have made it clear that the work, like Petronius' *Satyrica*, parodies motifs typical for the idealistic novel. Since in this case we know the entire plot, we can see too how the conventional structure of such texts is also travestied. In the idealistic novel, love at first sight and a pledge of faithfulness at the outset, then later the lovers' final reunion, form a framework for the adventures. The trials and tribulations of the ass are 'correspondingly' encased by two passionate nights with the maid Palaestra and the last rendezvous with the rich lady. Allusions to other idealistic motifs are found particularly in Lucius' period of captivity amongst the robbers, in the slave labour demanded of him by diverse masters, and in the frequent last-minute rescues; all of these are reminiscent of the experiences endured by the protagonists in narratives such as Xenophon's *Ephesiaca*. Thus the question arises once again as to whether the author intended his 'deheroization' of the idealistic novel's world to be something more than mere entertainment for the reader. The answer here too is closely connected with the man behind the work, and a look at the person of the author would seem to promise greater enlightenment than in the case of Petronius. As will be shown presently, the author of the *Ass Romance* is most likely to have been Lucian, and our knowledge of this writer is considerably more extensive than any information we have about Nero's *arbiter elegantiae*.

Very few scholars are today still of the opinion that the Lucius of Patrae named by Photius as the author actually wrote the *Ass Romance*. The first-person narrator, as we have just seen, uses this name himself, and it is hard to imagine author and comic hero bearing the same name even in a modern picaresque novel – the 'Tin Drum' player is not called Günter Grass! – let alone in an ancient romance. It is equally hard to believe that the versatile writer Lucian, to whom Photius and the manuscript tradition ascribe the epitome, would simply abridge the work of another author and pass the result off as his own writing. For the authorship of the original, on the other hand, he would seem to be the most likely candidate, having composed brilliant parodies of several other Greek literary genres – for example, the *True Stories*, to mention but one (see above, p. 14). Lucian lived, moreover, in exactly the same period to which the *Ass Romance*, on the basis of clues in the abridged text, can be dated: in the middle of the second century.

Besides his fondness for parodying, the writer and travelling rhetor Lucian (*c.* 120–80) from Samosata in Syria had one other thing in common with the author of the *Ass Romance*, something which has particular significance for our interpretation and which I shall try to elucidate. A predominant theme in Lucian's for the most part satirical writings is the exposure of the discrepancy between appearances and reality in all spheres of human life. In order to unmask social groups and individuals of varying kinds, even the Olympian gods, Lucian avails himself frequently of a means used by satirists of all ages: he observes men's doings from a vantage point which lies beyond reality. He has the central figures in his dialogues look down on the world from the moon or from the top of a pile of mountains, for example, or look up at it from the underworld; one observer of hidden vice watches in animal clothing – the Pythagoras of *Oneiros e alektruon* ('The Dream or The Cock') having been turned into this particular fowl. If we look at the *Ass Romance*, we find the transformed Lucius similarly in a position to observe a colourful range of human failings. He is made privy here to otherwise clandestine activities and behaviour, but this only because those involved really take him for an ass. Two examples of this are the sexual practices of the priests of the Syrian Goddess, who dally with a young farm-hand, and a rich lady's unfearing sexual preference for sodomy. The following conclusion therefore seems obvious: the author of the *Ass Romance* intended his parody of the idealistic novel at the same time as a satire on the *theatrum mundi*. His moral stance is expressed, as in Petronius, not explicitly, but in the way he presents things. And if we are ascribing authorship, Lucian is the obvious choice.

Satire, Platonism and mysteries: Apuleius, *Metamorphoses*

Whichever writer it was who actually did confront appearances and reality in a parody on the idealistic novel, his underlying intention was – in spite of the comic content of individual episodes – a serious one. It was, moreover, not only recognized as such by Apuleius, but also carried over by the Latin author into those passages of his *Metamorphoses* which correspond in their contents to sections of the original. In fact, Apuleius was at pains to render the intention clearly perceptible. In the Greek text events are described with the irony of distance, in the Latin the first-person narrator shows deep concern for the happenings he relates and constantly tries to draw in the reader too. He dramatizes events, strives to create on the one side overly comical effects, on the other overly sentimental pathos; he moralizes, psychologizes, turns descriptions into elaborate paintings. And in all this he betrays variously his plan to amplify the original and improve upon its narrative technique. The numerous short stories inserted into the plot of the *Ass Romance* underline this intention.

At one point in the *Metamorphoses* Apuleius even reveals quite openly that the 'ass's-eye view' is meant to represent in fictional form the 'spectacles' used by satirical observers of men and morals. In chapters 12 and 13 of book 9, the Latin Lucius describes the lowest point of human wretchedness witnessed by him, namely, in a mill, where slaves and animals are driven so cruelly that they are scarcely able to go on working. His comment:

> Nowhere was there any consolation for my tortured exist-
> ence, except one: I was revived by my innate curiosity, since
> everyone now took little account of my presence and freely
> did and said whatever they wished. That divine inventor of
> ancient poetry amongst the Greeks, desiring to portray a hero
> of the highest intelligence, was quite right to sing of a man
> who acquired the highest excellence by visiting many cities
> and learning to know various peoples. In fact, I now remem-
> ber the ass I was with thankful gratitude because, while I was
> concealed under his cover and schooled in a variety of for-
> tunes, he made me better-informed, if less intelligent.

As akin as the author of the *Ass Romance* and Apuleius are in their satirical view of the world, their respective assessments of man's chances of attaining true self-knowledge are very different. The Greek writer is pessimistic in his appraisal, as the workings of his protagonist's mind clearly show. Before losing his human shape, Lucius the man is not interested in real life, but in *paradoxa*, in magic and the world of illusion, and these are then, in the first part of the novel prior to his transformation, the very experiences he is confronted with in reality; the episode with the wineskins (see above, p. 74) illustrates this point well. The instant he himself is put under a spell, however, the *paradoxa* suddenly vanish. He no longer sees the world of illusions he had been so keen to enter into before his metamorphosis, but instead the everyday realities of life for his fellow men. They are now the ones who are taken in by an illusion, believing Lucius to be an ass and revealing their true natures in front of him. The logical consequence of this is that, after returning to his human form, Lucius loses the insight he had gained while an ass. As quadruped he had seen quite clearly that the rich, passionate lady lusted solely after his animal flesh and that she could therefore only afford to reveal her true self behind closed doors. Now, as a man again, Lucius really imagines that the same lady will find him more desirable in his human form. The lady, however, merely remarks that he is no longer physically equal to her needs, since he now has, as she puts it, the body of a 'monkey'; without further ado she has him thrown out on to the street, naked as he is (56). Once back in his human shape, then, the Lucius of the *Ass Romance* sees things as falsely as he had done before his first transformation, when he was still eager to experience magic and witchcraft. In world literature as a whole there are probably not very many scenes in which man's perceptive abilities are questioned with such merciless cynicism as in this, on the surface undoubtedly amusing, but deep down rather disturbing, passage.

Apuleius, by contrast, was clearly of the opinion that there are ways by which man can come to recognize his true nature: through religion and philosophy. The potential of religiosity in this respect is shown to us in the conclusion of the *Metamorphoses*: Apuleius' Lucius, as yet still an ass, flees at the end of book 10 from the theatre to a secluded beach and prays during the night to Isis (beginning of book 11), entreating that she return him to his former shape; in a dream the goddess tells him how his wish is to be fulfilled. The next day, following her instructions, he works his way through the crowd of believers watching a large procession in honour of the goddess, and eats the roses on a garland which is wound around a cult instrument in the hands of the high priest. The rest of the book gives an account first of the transformed Lucius' initiation into the mysteries of Isis; there then follows a stay in Rome. The first-person narrator suddenly refers to himself here as the 'man from Madaurus', so that author and narrative 'I' are for the reader now one and the same. He is initiated into the cult of Osiris and finally enters one of the colleges of the god's priests.

Lucius' devotion to Isis also provides him with a belated explanation for his transformation into an ass. In the words of the high priest: 'On the slippery path of headstrong youth you plunged into slavish pleasures and reaped the perverse reward of your ill-starred curiosity' (11.15). It comes as something of a surprise for the reader to hear that the sufferings of the ass were a form of divine punishment. In the part of the story prior to Lucius' transformation into the ass, the appeasement of his 'slavish' desires – obviously an allusion to the passionate nights spent with the maidservant (Apuleius calls her Photis) – and his lively interest in witchcraft are nowhere termed an offence against religion. There is then quite evidently a certain contradiction here: in his recapitulation of events before his metamorphosis the first-person narrator is apparently unaware that he has committed any outrage, and not until the end of the novel are we given the theological interpretation.

However, in books 1–3 of the *Metamorphoses*, which tell the story leading up to Lucius' first transformation, there are numerous hints pointing to the explanation later given. We have, for example, the scene in the house of Lucius' aunt Byrrhaena in which he examines a marble sculpture; it represents Actaeon spying on Diana as she prepares to bathe and being turned into a stag for his audacity (2.4–5). This could be read as a cryptic warning for Lucius. Or we have the parallel between the preparatory instructions given to Lucius by Photis before he is allowed to watch her mistress at work (3.15) and several of the motifs used in the chapters describing Lucius' ritual initiation (11.22 ff.). Photis explicitly adopts the pose of a mystagogue, telling Lucius not to say a word to anyone about what he will soon see and singing the praises of her mistress's powers in words otherwise used only to celebrate a goddess. Readers familiar with the contemporary mystery cults were supposed to begin to suspect here that serious religious initiation rites are about to be perverted. To say of a witch that the elements are 'enslaved' by her (3.15.7) is blasphemous, as is later confirmed when Lucius says the same of Isis in his hymn to the goddess: 'the elements are your slaves' (11.25.3).

Curiosity as sacrilege in a religious context is a thought to which the reader is gradually attuned, not only at the beginning of the novel, but also in its centre-piece: in the tale of Cupid and Psyche (4.28–6.24). This tells us how the beautiful princess Psyche, whose goddess-like appearance causes a wrathful Venus to hound her, is taken, as prescribed by an oracle, to the top of a lonely crag and left there alone to await an unknown beast-bridegroom; a gentle wind carries the maiden off to a magnificent, but completely uninhabited, palace and there, night for night, she shares Cupid's bed. She is, however, unaware of her husband's identity. The god wishes to remain anonymous and forbids her to look at him, but curiosity – and Psyche's two sisters, who pay her three visits and add fuel to the flame – drive her to ignore Cupid's warnings. She gazes upon him one night by the light of a lamp, and he punishes her by taking flight. After a failed attempt to kill herself, Psyche begins to search for Cupid, the sight of whom has filled her with burning, passionate love. She turns to Venus, but the goddess behaves towards her as would any prospective nasty mother-in-law, imposing on her three tasks which this Cinderella can only manage to complete with the help of animals and plants. Venus then sends her off to Hades to fetch a box from Proserpina; although warned again not to be inquisitive, Psyche opens the box and falls into a death-like sleep. Cupid rouses her and Jupiter grants her immortality in order that she can marry the god of love; their union results in the birth of a daughter, *Voluptas* ('Pleasure').

The tale was very probably Apuleius' own creation, following the outlines of plots used in the idealistic novel and borrowing from a variety of other genres to embellish the narrative. The thought that springs to mind on reading this is that the novella was meant to be taken symbolically – an assumption already voiced in late antiquity – and countless such interpretations have been put forward. To enumerate all of these would be to overload this introduction, but the most convincing one is the Platonic reading. The description of Psyche's path from the moment curiosity causes her to err until she finally attains immortality is clearly, sometimes even literally, an echo of those passages in Plato's *Phaedrus* which relate in mythical images the journeyings of the soul (*psuche*) before it is allowed to contemplate the divine. The affinity in theme between Psyche's vain attempts to hold back the fugitive Cupid (*Met.* 5.24.1) and the fall of the soul, which tries to go with the god but cannot fly for the weight of its vice (*Phaedr.* 248c) is quite unmistakable. There are also obvious parallels between Psyche's burning desire for Cupid and that of the soul for the divine (*Met.* 5.23/*Phaedr.* 251e), and in the readiness of both to do the work of slaves if only they can thus satisfy their desires. It is quite feasible that Apuleius' narrative was meant to open up for readers a further, higher field of knowing, another indication of this being that the Venus of the novella can be linked to the Isis of book 11.

Man's thirst for knowledge, where expressed in the form of *curiositas*, then, is rated within the *Metamorphoses* of Apuleius sometimes as negative, sometimes as positive, depending on the context. Where it is judged negative – in books 1–3, book 11 and in the tale of Cupid and Psyche – *curiositas* is far removed from an approach towards human problems that seeks knowledge of the highest truths in the teachings of Plato and in the mysteries of Isis and Osiris. Where it is judged positive – in books 4–10 – it is the frame of mind which makes it possible fully to perceive the difference between appearances and reality in varying spheres. However, there seems to be little point in asking whether Apuleius believed these two aspects – the philosophical-theological and the satirical – to be compatible and therefore deliberately combined them, or whether it perhaps escaped his notice that his changes to the ending of the Greek *Metamorphoseis* entailed a contradiction in the use of the term 'curiositas'. For this reason discussions of the work which talk of its 'ideological unity' ought not to imply that the central intention of the author lies exclusively in his theological and philosophical teachings and thus overlook the satirical content.

Moral satire hand in hand with pious faith in mystery cults, burlesque sketches alongside of edifying devotion to religion – these are combinations which characterize Apuleius' novel and as such may not quite satisfy the literary and aesthetic tastes of some readers. However, one factor must be remembered here: in the second century, when this work was written, the Roman Empire was exposed to and greatly influenced by a confusing spectrum of ideologies. These ranged from belief in the old gods to philosophical doctrines, from mystery cults to the Christian faith. An inevitable consequence for the individual was the problematic decision as to which religion or philosophy he or she should espouse as their mainstay in life. The *Metamorphoses* of Apuleius unmistakably reflects this situation. We know that the author himself showed an interest in several of the spiritual trends prevalent in his time. Born around the year 125 in Madaurus, a town in the Roman province

Africa proconsularis (North Africa), he wrote a number of Platonic works, called himself proudly a 'philosophus Platonicus' and was initiated into various mystery cults in Greece and Asia Minor during extensive travels there. Platonism and mysteries represent only two of this man's many interests. Besides being a high priest of Aesculapius in Carthage, he was a renowned rhetorician there, and, in addition to Platonic writings and declamations, he wrote poems, historical works and treatises on science, arithmetic and music. Another of his interests – the occult – even landed him in a court of law. The speech he wrote in his own defence survives – the *Apologia*, a brilliant piece of rhetoric; it shows him to be guided in his thought and manifold scholarly pursuits by a movement which first began to enjoy wider popularity when Apuleius was travelling in the Greek-speaking world: the so-called Second Sophistic. The same movement was to influence the authors of the three most notable extant Greek novels, to which we now turn in what will be the final chapter of this introduction.

5

THE IDEALISTIC NOVEL
IN THE AGE OF THE
SECOND SOPHISTIC

In many respects comparable to the age of humanism in early modern times, the intellectual movement known as the 'Second Sophistic' flowered from the beginning of the second to the middle of the third century. It is characterized principally by the demand that sound rhetorical training precede any kind of higher education, and by the choice of Classical Greece rather than the Hellenistic period as its source of literary models. Rhetors now held prominent positions in cultural life as school directors, itinerant lecturers and public orators. This was a development greatly furthered by the establishment under the emperor Vespasian (69–79) of state-funded chairs of rhetoric, and by the general philhellenic disposition of the second-century Caesars. Anyone active in the literary field during this period had, then, been taught by a rhetor how to write a prose distinctive in its use of rhetorical figures, complex periods and studied poetical expressions – a style first cultivated at the end of the fifth century BC by the sophist Gorgias. Stress was also given in such studies to elaborate descriptive pieces and digressions on the obscurest of subjects; these were to be woven into compositions.

We know of five Greek novelists who were influenced by the Second Sophistic: Iamblichus, Achilles Tatius, Longus, Heliodorus, and the author of *Herpyllis*. Their debt to this cultural tradition manifests itself clearly in their sophisticated, highly-wrought style, in a tendency to flaunt their literary, scientific, geographical and ethnical knowledge, and in their striving both to furnish descriptions of places and objects with realistic detail, and to work subtle psychological observations into their character portrayals. In this last respect these five Greek writers display a mastery previously unattained in the idealistic novel. Their skilled characterizing puts them on a par with the authors of the comic-realistic novels. Like the latter, those writers schooled by the Second Sophistic were able to create men and women of flesh and blood, rather than puppets of the type that populate the stage in Xenophon of Ephesus' *Ephesiaca*. They knew how to bring the fictional world in which their characters live closer to reality, or at least as close as the traditionally idealized world in this type of novel could be allowed to come.

Wallowing in lurid effects: Iamblichus, *Babyloniaca*

Exactly how far Iamblichus, the author of the *Babyloniaca* ('A Babylonian Story'), can be compared to the writers of comic-realistic novels in his use of realistic elements for his characters and plot is, unfortunately, impossible to tell. The text itself – written some time at the beginning of the last third of the second century – survives only in a large number of short quotations and in three fragments which are each roughly the length of one chapter. All we know of the text as a whole is what Photius tells us in his summary (cod. 94). The autobiographical data given by Iamblichus some-where in the novel at the end of a digression on the mysteries of Aphrodite and on various kinds of magic, are reminiscent of the information offered at the end of the *Ass Romance* by the first-person narrator, Lucius of Patrae, as to his family and occupation. Iamblichus describes himself as a Babylonian who is familiar with the magic arts and has had a Greek education; he maintains that he had predicted the beginning and the outcome of the war waged by Lucius Verus against the Parthian King Vologaeses III (in the years 162–165). Iamblichus thus makes himself part of the exotic world in which his novel takes place, much the same as does the self-declared story-writer and author of the *Ass Romance*. His words ought therefore to be treated with scepticism in regard to their historical value, as must the biographical details found in a note in the margin of a Photius manuscript. Here we are told that Iamblichus was originally from Syria and that a Babylonian had taught him the language, magic arts and customs of his native land, and had also passed on to him the 'Babylonian Story'. This rather dubious information was possibly extracted from the novel itself and sounds very much like feigned authentication for the historicity of the work, serving, then, the same purpose as the sketch we are given in the *Ass Romance* of its narrator. One further marginal note tells us that Iamblichus was a capable rhetor and this seems, by contrast, to be reliable information. There survive two lengthy samples of his Neosophistic representational skills. One is a description of the Babylonian king's magnificent procession, the other a speech made in court by a husband prosecuting his wife, who has admitted that she committed adultery with a slave in a dream. The digressions mentioned in Photius' summary point to the same intellectual background as these displays of rhetorical brilliance.

Photius' account covers sixteen books of the novel which, according to the *Suda*, was divided into thirty-nine (another reading gives thirty-five) books in all. Given the uncommonly large number of single episodes in the plot as we know it, and its sheer length, it would be very hard to offer a concise outline of the story in the space available here. A synopsis of a synopsis would in any case be of questionable value. The central figures of the novel were Rhodanes and his wife Sinonis, a couple forced to flee when cruel King Garmus of Babylon decided that he wanted to marry Sinonis himself. At various places in Mesopotamia – the time is an age before Persian rule there – the two underwent a series of adventures. These were strung loosely together or related in parallel accounts, much in the same way as Xenophon of Ephesus presents the tribulations of Anthia and Habrocomes (see above, pp. 1–6). In another respect the *Babyloniaca* seems also to have been reminiscent of Lollianus' *Phoenicica*, in that the author took great delight in jarring effects and scenes in which a liberal amount of blood flowed. In the course of the plot readers were confronted with a robber who ate human flesh, a dog that fed on corpses, bees and a fly that killed with one sting, and a king who would cut off ears and noses as punishment or bury the alleged miscreants alive and who danced with flute girls around the cross upon which Rhodanes was crucified. Of the more conventional motifs apparent death and (attempted) suicide occurred particularly frequently.

The prominence given to this morbid element – there was even a digression on the regulations and procedures to be observed by the public executioner – undoubtedly formed one essential feature of the author's characterization of the Eastern world as cruel and barbarous. However, a similar smell of the grave permeates the surviving excerpts from Petronius' *Satyrica* with the significance almost of a leitmotif, and in the *Ass Romance* Lucius' experiences after his transformation consist mainly of sadistic torments. We should therefore not rule out the possibility that, in contrast to their role in other extant idealistic novels, pain and death played an important part in the picture Iamblichus presented of the world, just as they do in the disillusioning portrayal of life found in the comic-realistic novels. Photius sheds no light on this point, but instead baffles us once again. In the sixteenth of – according to the *Suda* – at least thirty-five books, Photius read about the couple's joyous reunion and Rhodanes' ascent to the throne of Babylon. What came after this (presuming that the number of books named in the *Suda* is correct and that Photius was not using an epitome) is only one of the many questions posed by Iamblichus' *Babyloniaca*, and our limited knowledge of the text remains a stumbling-block in the search for answers.

Adding the human touch: Achilles Tatius, *Leucippe and Clitophon*

Turning now to the works of Achilles Tatius, Longus and Heliodorus, we come to those Greek prose narratives which have exerted the most widespread and lasting influence on modern European literature. Achilles Tatius' novel *Leucippe and Clitophon* probably enjoyed a certain popularity for some while after its composition; we have papyrus fragments which date from the late second to the early fourth century, and the youngest of these seems to be from an epitome. The novel is generally believed to have been written in the second half of the second century, an assumption based on the text transmission and on certain indications within the work itself. Of its author we know – the familiar story – next to nothing; even his correct name is not absolutely certain. Some of the medieval manuscripts call him 'Statius' and this cannot necessarily be dismissed as mere misappropriation of the 's' in 'Achilles'. Nevertheless, 'Tatius' seems preferable (if we assume that the name is not Latin in origin, but Egyptian: from the god 'Thoth') as it is more than once recorded that the author hailed from Alexandria. The *Suda* attributes to Achilles Tatius not only the novel, but in addition works on the heavenly sphere, etymology and on the lives of famous men. Of these other writings there survive only fragments of the text on astronomy, and although the style in which they are written differs considerably from the language of *Leucippe and Clitophon*, we have no reason to reject them as the work of this many-sided Neosophist.

Leucippe and Clitophon is the only fully extant idealistic novel narrated in the first person. It begins with the narrator's account of how in the Phoenician city of Sidon (the original title of the work was possibly *Phoenicica*) he comes across a painting which depicts the abduction of Europa. He examines it closely and a remark escapes his lips on the power of the boy Eros. Hearing this exclamation, the hero of the novel, Clitophon, strikes up a conversation with the narrator and, in a grove under the shade of plane trees, tells him the story of his life up until his marriage to the beautiful Leucippe. Like Chariton's *Callirhoe*, the novel is divided into eight books. The central motifs of the plot, which follows the conventional generic pattern, are distributed over four blocks. The two outer ones each contain in two books (1/2 and 7/8) the start of the love-story and the events leading directly to its happy ending. Within this framework there are two sets of adventures proper, the experiences *en route* (3/4) being separated from the tests of loyalty to which the lovers are subjected through the advances of others (5/6).

Two whole books are needed to cover the beginning of the couple's love, because the obligatory love at first sight befalls only the man in this case. Before Leucippe actually returns Clitophon's love, readers follow for some time the various approaches he (now himself the first-person narrator) makes, his suffering and his consultations with a friend and with the slave Satyrus. The manner in which Clitophon's wishes are then fulfilled comes as a complete surprise: in the middle of book 2 Leucippe is persuaded to await him one night in her chamber, and their premarital union is only prevented because the girl's mother bursts into the room at the last minute. Clitophon manages to escape without being recognized, but is afraid that there will be trouble and so decides to flee with his beloved. Accompanied by Satyrus and two friends, the couple board a ship bound for Alexandria.

The scene of books 3 and 4 is for the most part Egypt. The travellers are very soon separated for a while by a storm and ensuing shipwreck. The lovers are captured in the Nile Delta by robbers who decide to sacrifice Leucippe by way of expiation. Clitophon, who is freed by soldiers shortly after being taken prisoner, must watch from the other side of a broad trench while Leucippe is disembowelled and put into a coffin. Not until the following night are he and the reader told that Satyrus and one of the two friends had also been captured by the robbers after reaching land and had themselves undertaken to perform the sacrifice; this they had merely pretended to do, using an actor's trick sword with a sliding blade and a bag of animal entrails tied around Leucippe's waist. The true story behind a similar ordeal – at the beginning of book 5 Leucippe is carried off and seemingly decapitated by her new abductors – is only revealed after a considerably longer interval. The incident takes place on a ship that has left the harbour, with Clitophon hot in pursuit on another vessel. Convinced that Leucippe really is dead, he returns for a time to Egypt, where he meets a rich widow from Ephesus, Melite, and promises to marry her; accompanying her to her home, he finds Leucippe there, working as a slave on Melite's country estate.

Most of the third block (books 5 and 6) is devoted to the account of how Clitophon resists consummation of his marriage to Melite and how Leucippe is pestered by Melite's enamoured first husband. His wife had wrongly believed him dead, and he now suddenly returns home from the journey during which he had purportedly been drowned. The husband hounds Clitophon with his hatred and thus affords Melite at one point the opportunity to help her second husband out of a difficult situation. She is consequently able to persuade Clitophon – once again to our astonishment – to sleep with her. At the beginning of book 7 a plot instigated by the husband leads Clitophon to believe for the third time that Leucippe has been killed. In his grief he publicly accuses himself of the murder and is about to be tortured when – not unlike the hermit in Weber's opera *Der Freischütz* – the priest of Artemis of Ephesus comes on the scene. His appearance signals that an embassy to the goddess has arrived, and the punitive measures against Clitophon must therefore be suspended. Amongst the embassy is Leucippe's father, and the path now begins to be cleared of all complications, allowing the lovers finally to marry. The happy event is preceded by a scene which rounds off all the novel's surprises in worthy fashion. Melite and Leucippe are forced to undergo a trial by ordeal, the one to prove her marital fidelity, the other to prove her virginity. Not only is the girl found to be intact, but the wife too comes out as innocent. Melite owes her acquittal, of course, to a technicality: her first, unwitting husband, who has accused her of adultery, words his challenge in such a way that the period for which she must swear that she has been faithful is confined to his absence from Ephesus.

This brief synopsis has given a little more weight to those elements of the plot which seem to link _Leucippe and Clitophon_ to the comic-realistic novels. To consider first the form of the narrative, Achilles Tatius, like Petronius and the author of the _Ass Romance_, chose to present his story in the first person. Thus the reader experiences events through the eyes of the narrator-hero and can more easily identify with him and the other characters. This allows the author, as will be demonstrated below when we consider his skilled characterizations, to render the story more realistic; the very fact that the first-person narrator relates not (pseudo-)historical events, but things he has himself recently experienced, makes his narrative more immediate. Moreover, replacing 'authorial' with 'personal' narrative means that the limited perspective open to the narrative 'I', who is not able to survey the whole picture when he is actually involved himself, can be used to heighten the suspense. While Clitophon does – particularly in the second half of the novel – frequently relate events which he can only know about retrospectively, there are also the gripping scenes in which Leucippe is seemingly butchered or decapitated and the narrator, as he talks, is convinced that this has all really happened. The story-teller's restricted vision here means that the reader is all the more shocked. As we shall see below, this technique – one also found in comic-realistic novels (cf. the wineskin episode in the _Ass Romance_, above p. 74) – is employed even more extensively by Heliodorus.

Another narrative device often used by Achilles Tatius is one he would have become acquainted with during his studies in rhetoric. In the middle of an account of facts presented in relatively simple style, he likes to insert elaborate feats of language skill. These take the form of detailed descriptions of people or objects, short mythographical or scientific discourses – for example on the hippopotamus or the crocodile (4.2 and 19) – brief psychologizing comments, or discussions on the pros and cons of issues that are only of marginal relevance to the plot. One such display of stylistic brilliance is the description of a storm at the beginning of book 2, and this passage provides us with a parallel and a possible means of classification for the one surviving remnant of an otherwise unknown novel. In a second-century papyrus fragment (PDublin inv. C 3) the lover of a girl named Herpyllis is at sea and avails himself of several rhetorical figures to describe the raging of the elements. This would seem to indicate that the novel was likewise written by an author of the Second Sophistic. The protagonist of what is now usually entitled *Herpyllis* was in all probability, like Clitophon, the narrator too. The novelist clearly also resembled Achilles Tatius in a fondness for bringing his learning to the fore, because the description of the thunder and gales is amplified with meteorological and scientific details.

The scholarly world has, even in recent times, always tended to look down upon such interludes because they are not acceptable as poetry in the classicist's understanding of the word. This judgement even included the *descriptiones* used by Ovid, one of antiquity's greatest poets. And yet in Achilles Tatius the presence of a literary intention is manifest in the mere fact that his descriptions, digressions, theoretical essays and debates are introduced at points of rest in the plot. Clitophon's discussion with friends on the respective merits of women and boys as lovers, for instance, comes at the end of book 2, closing the love-story proper.

In the same passage Clitophon describes at length a deep kiss and makes observations on the female orgasm (2.37), and this exemplifies an aspect of Achilles Tatius' writing that again seems to link his work to the comic-realistic novels. He strives to represent exactly the inner thought processes of individual characters, showing at the same time an interest in the theoretical psychology of the case, particularly where eroticism is concerned. The markedly realistic view of human sexual activities given in the comic-realistic novels – one example being the lengthy description of a 'wrestling-match' between the first-person narrator and the maid Palaestra (Gr. 'wrestling-school') in the *Ass Romance* (*Onos* 9 f.) – is characteristic of this branch of the genre. In the idealistic novels of Chariton and Xenophon of Ephesus, by contrast, the erotic element had been restricted in the main to falling in love at first sight, pledging undying faithfulness and marrying after stout resistance to all temptations. Achilles Tatius, however, now ventures a modification of this austere pattern, with characters who are, after all, only human. He has love smite only the hero at first sight, and the girl must then be conquered in courtship manoeuvres which are depicted with a skilled psychological subtlety reminiscent of Ovid's *Ars Amatoria*. Sex before marriage may be prevented at the last minute, but is here at least within the realms of possibility, and the hero is, under exceptional circumstances (he is being held prisoner), allowed an infidelity. The woman who begs tearfully of Clitophon this 'once-doesn't-count' favour, is not simply 'wanton', as Rohde and others have indignantly called her; she is in fact one of the most subtly drawn characters in ancient narrative literature. And when the first-person narrator says that the act would not be 'a marital one but was rather a remedy for an ailing soul' (5.27.2), he almost seems to foreshadow modern psychotherapy. The author, at any rate, can turn a blind eye and have Melite's behaviour sanctioned in a trial by ordeal at the end of the novel.

It is all too easy for us to laugh now at this writer's doubtlessly quite serious efforts to analyse the emotions of his characters by adding theorizing comments, as the following example might tempt us to do:

Then at last my tears came and granted my eyes their grief. For just as when a bruise from a blow to the body does not rise at once, and the blow at first creates no mottled flower on the skin, but shortly afterwards it rises to the surface; and just as when a person slashed by a boar's tusk looks for the wound and cannot see it, for it goes down deep, and its slow-motion effect is hidden, but suddenly a thin white line appears, harbinger of blood, and after a pause blood arrives and flows abundantly – just so the soul struck by an arrow of grief shot from a story is already wounded and cut, but because the injury occurred with such velocity, the wound did not open at once, and the tears from the eyes followed far behind; for a tear is the blood from a wound in the soul. As the tooth of sorrow slowly gnaws at the heart, the soul's wound breaks open, in the eyes a door opens for tears, and a short while later they flow out. So it was that the first hearing of his story, striking my soul like an arrow's sudden impact, left me silent and stopped my tears at their source; but afterwards they flowed, when my soul's tense attention to its shock had relaxed.

(7.4.3–6)

Considering how limited the possibilities were for going beyond the boundaries set by the genre, we must give Achilles Tatius all the more credit for having tried to render the often almost sterile world of the idealistic novel more human.

Sexual psychology and bucolic paradise: Longus, *Daphnis and Chloe*

While Achilles Tatius went so far as to replace the conventional motif of mutual 'love at first sight' with a gradual development of erotic relations between hero and heroine that took up one quarter of his work, Longus ventured considerably further in his *Daphnis and Chloe* (*Lesbiaca*): he stretched the coming together of the two lovers over the entire plot. Here, then, we seem to have one exponent of the genre competing with another, the motif in question being such a very conspicuous one, and everything points to Longus as the conscious imitator trying at the same time to outdo his predecessor. This at least provides us with a fairly reliable *terminus post quem* for the novel, which is otherwise extremely difficult to date. We may place it at the earliest towards the end of the second century, a dating also suggested by various associative links with contemporary works of art, as well as stylistic and thematic similarities to other literature of the age. It cannot, on the other hand, be assigned to a period too far into the third century, because it seems to form a sort of midpoint between the novels of Achilles Tatius and Heliodorus. The *Aethiopica* – written, as will be shown below, before the end of the first half of the third century – appears to be a deliberate break with the liberal eroticism displayed in Achilles Tatius and Longus. It is, at the same time, closer to the latter's pastoral novel, in that Heliodorus too presents the traditional myth of salvation with its own custom-made paradise as background. Longus' work, we may then assume, was written around the turn of the second to the third century. Of the author himself we know nothing except that he probably came from the island of Lesbos, the scene of the novel, and that he perhaps belonged to the Pompeii Longi, a family recorded in inscriptions there.

Daphnis and Chloe opens with a motif also used in *Leucippe and Clitophon*, one which is similarly found at the beginning of the novel. While out hunting near Mytilene in a grove sacred to the Nymphs, the author sees a picture which provides not only the chance opportunity for him to unfold his tale, but which even depicts already the entire story of his novel. It awakes in him the desire to compete, as literary artist, with the painter. As we may expect of an author of the Second Sophistic, the competition is also to be one of form, with Longus parading all the rhetorical devices at his disposal and illuminating his show-pieces – these include magnificent nature scenes – with as much colour as possible.

Daphnis and Chloe were both exposed at birth by their respective parents and suckled in the one case by a goat, in the other by a ewe; each is found by a different shepherd and brought up as one of the family. Later, the 15-year-old Daphnis and 13-year-old Chloe tend their grazing goats and sheep together and begin to fall in love. This is the start of inevitable difficulties for the two young innocents in their mutual striving to translate into active expressions of affection the longing they each have for a closer relationship. Their plight represents the 'travel adventures' motif in Longus' novel. It may not be a journey to far-off lands that the two undertake, but it is an equally 'hazardous' one: they travel through the strange terrain of the soul and experience what is in store there for two young people discovering, step by step, physical love. The different stages of this 'journey' consist in the new insights gained from educative observation, from instruction by other persons, and from failed ventures. Their stock of knowledge increases steadily as the seasons take their course and love matures: 'Daphnis and Chloe embark on a journey not in space, but in time' (B. Reardon, 'The Greek Novel', p. 301).

Sometimes helpful, sometimes threatening, the encounters between the couple and the rest of the world are, as far as the dangers are concerned, reminiscent of the experiences had by the heroes of other idealistic novels. In the first of the work's four books, Phoenician pirates landing on the coast of Lesbos abduct Daphnis and a herd of cattle; in book 2 a company of rich young men from Methymna force Chloe to go with them on their ship. In both cases rescue comes at the last minute. In the first, Chloe's syrinx-playing causes all the cattle on board the pirates' departing vessel to jump from one side of the deck into the sea, and the ship capsizes (shipwreck motif!); in the second, Pan, god of shepherds, sends terrifying apparitions to prevent the ship from leaving. There are other episodes also familiar from the other novels, with a rival attempting to win the hero or the heroine for him- or herself. In book 1 it is a shepherd who wants Chloe to love him, and in book 4 the toadying male friend of the estate-owner's son who takes a passionate interest in Daphnis, while another shepherd carries off Chloe. Again, these threats to the couple's love are no more than short episodes, basically harmless in their outcome and only very distantly related to the mortal dangers faced in most cases by the persecuted protagonists in novels like that of Xenophon of Ephesus. For Daphnis and Chloe everything happens in an idyllic country world, the tranquillity of which is guarded by protecting gods. The serene, cheerful atmosphere of the 'adventure' section is, in the final happy outcome, quite appropriately complemented by a motif which Longus borrowed from New Comedy: in two surprise recognition scenes Daphnis and Chloe are each identified as offspring of rich citizens from Mytilene. Immediately afterwards, the two are married.

The 'adventures' proper are of far less significance for the plot of *Daphnis and Chloe* than comparable happenings in other idealistic novels. Their function here is more that of a subplot. The main line of action consists instead of alternating advances and setbacks on the difficult path towards the fulfilment of love. This progress is described in full detail by Longus, from the minute when Chloe feels the first flutterings after seeing Daphnis naked (1.13) until their wedding-night, which closes the novel. The outstanding moments on their voyage of sensual discovery – these being episodes which again call to mind thematically similar passages from the comic-realistic novels – are the two following. First, the sequence of scenes to which the old, experienced shepherd Philetas gives rise with his lessons on the nature of Love. Having been told by him that only 'a kiss and an embrace and lying down together with naked bodies' (2.7.7) can help against the power of Love, Daphnis and Chloe try out these remedies one by one – the lying down only after some hesitation – and, for a day at least, hold them to be 'the limit of love's satisfaction' (2.11). Second, these attempts having brought them no further forward, a dissatisfied Daphnis tries to imitate what 'the rams do to the ewes . . . and the he-goats to the she-goats'. He simply clasps Chloe from behind, and this too fails to bring any improvement (3.14). However, help comes unexpectedly from Lycaenion, a young woman from town who is married to a farmer older than herself. She is in love with Daphnis and secretly observes the scene just described; she now seizes the chance to fulfil her own desires by giving the youth an exhaustive lesson in love-making. Daphnis only refrains from passing his new knowledge on to Chloe immediately, waiting instead until their wedding-night, because Lycaenion frightens him with a warning about the physical and emotional side-effects defloration will have on his chosen partner (3.15–20).

In this day and age it need hardly be pointed out that these and other episodes make Longus' novel a masterpiece in terms of psychological perception. This is, in any case, a verdict already reached over 150 years ago by one of the greatest minds of the period – Goethe. On the 9th, 18th and 20th of March 1831, in conversations with his friend Eckermann, he praised enthusiastically the 'intelligence, art and tastefulness' of this pastoral novel ('by comparison with which good old Virgil falls back a little') and remarked of the erotic explorations 'that here the greatest affairs of mankind are articulated'; he recommended that the work be read once a year so that one could 'learn from it again and again and sense anew the impression of its great beauty'. It is therefore all the more surprising that German classical scholars of the Wilamowitz era and later times were almost unanimous in their horrified contempt for the 'sexual perversity' and 'sultry lasciviousness' of the 'squalid, near pornographic sphere' in which the novel is set (R. Helm, *Der antike Roman*, p. 51). This could be excused in view of the strait-laced attitudes generated by the age of Wilhelm II, but there is more to come: Goethe's opinion was deplored with smug, schoolmasterly presumption as a 'strange misjudgement', and these pronouncements were then to colour scholars' picture of Longus through into the 1960s.

If from that point onwards studies of *Daphnis and Chloe* tended to busy themselves with attempts to explain the novel's pastoral setting and the role played by divine powers, this was noticeably paralleled by an apparent indifference towards the erotic scenes. These were now more or less left aside without any further comment. Moreover, the line of interpretation taking ancient novels to be propaganda for mystery cults (here those of Dionysus and/or Eros) found unusually wide acceptance in, of all cases, that of Longus' pastoral romance. In the light of the moral indignation which the work had formerly aroused, this would seem to be the result of a shift to another extreme. Nevertheless, the question of Longus' intention in his coupling of the bucolic world with the idealistic novel's traditional pattern of action is absolutely legitimate and plays a key role in any understanding of *Daphnis and Chloe*. Here we have a prose author writing at the beginning of the third century who avails himself of motifs typical for the bucolic poetry cultivated by the Alexandrian court poet Theocritus in the third century BC, and who sometimes even alludes literally to specific verses of this kind. The sociological circumstances which govern the production of literature obviously having changed in the centuries between the two writers, Longus must have had a particular reason for doing this.

Bernd Effe should be given the credit for finding a plausible answer here. In a brilliant study ('Longos: Zur Funktionsgeschichte der Bukolik in der römischen Kaiserzeit') he interprets the idyllic world of *Daphnis and Chloe*, where the two shepherds live in childlike innocence and the gods guarantee peace, as a contrast to the realities of urban life in Imperial times, the latter a culture felt to be over-civilized and morally depraved. As was shown above (pp. 30 ff.), the novel as a genre had always been designed to compensate readers for their dissatisfaction in everyday life by offering them a contrasting world. Here, the alternative ideal is given concrete form, in a sphere outside the towns. Effe quite rightly stresses, however, that the description of the serene life led by country shepherds, as idealized as it may be, also contains typical town-dweller notions of culture and civilization. These become increasingly prominent above all towards the end of the novel. Daphnis and Chloe specifically choose to celebrate their wedding in the country and live the rest of their lives mostly as shepherds (4.39). None the less, they are not averse to their new, unexpected wealth, although money and possessions customarily rate as negative items in most town–country comparisons. Also very significant in this respect is a remark made by the author when Chloe first appears dressed town-style for her wedding: 'Then you could learn what beauty is like, when it is properly presented' (4.32.1).

The motif of the opposites town and country is paralleled in abstract terms by the polarity between *nature* (*phusis*) and *skilled art* (*techne*), a theme treated by Longus on different levels. Landscape, for example, is a vehicle for the illustration of the reciprocal relation between nature and art on the spatial level. His garden descriptions are the unmistakable expression of an ideal, one which is formulated with particular succinctness in the description of Chloe just quoted above: the refinement of *phusis* through *techne*. The most important insight imparted by Longus is one he shares, although perhaps not consciously so, with Ovid: as the *Ars amatoria* also teaches, erotic perfection too is only possible when nature and art are combined in joint effort. The scenes in which Daphnis and Chloe gradually learn the art of love can unquestionably be read as an *ars amatoria* in narrative form. And in a closed society like that of the second/third century, such a 'course of instruction' could, if at all, only take place in the country. There is, then, a quite simple explanation for Longus' choice of a bucolic setting: it is, as it were, the classroom.

Longus makes it clear from the start that he intends not only to entertain, but also to educate his reader. He states in the prologue that his novel will be something for mankind to possess and enjoy. It will cure the sick, comfort the distressed, stir the memory of those who have loved, and educate those who haven't.

This is quite clearly an allusion to Thucydides' declared intention that his *History* will be 'a possession for ever'. If any of the Greek novels can fulfil such an aspiration, then it is that of Longus, which still numbers today beside Petronius' *Satyrica* and Apuleius' *Metamorphoses* amongst the great narrative works of world literature.

Acme of narrative technique: Heliodorus, *Aethiopica*

By contrast, Heliodorus' *Aethiopica* ('An Ethiopian Story'), which was the most successful of all Greek prose narratives in terms of formative influence on later authors – and this most tangibly in the early stages of the development of the modern European novel – none the less probably does not hold as much direct appeal for today's readers as do the narratives of Apuleius, Petronius and Longus. In its contents the text represents a return to the type of idealistic novel written in late Hellenistic and early Imperial times, and its significance for literary history lies above all in its outward, technical aspects. The author's highly developed art of representation surpasses the earlier performances of all other Greek novelists in this respect. A device which is particularly characteristic of Heliodorus' technique, namely the shrouding of events in mystery, is put to use with great effect right at the beginning of the novel. By way of example here are the first lines of this famous opening scene.

The smile of daybreak was just beginning to brighten the sky, the sunlight to catch the hilltops, when a group of men in brigand gear peered over the mountain that overlooks the place where the Nile flows into the sea at the mouth that men call the Heracleotic. They stood there for a moment, scanning the expanse of sea beneath them: first they gazed out over the ocean, but as there was nothing sailing there that held out hope of spoil and plunder, their eyes were drawn to the beach nearby. This is what they saw . . .

The mysterious sight which presents itself to the eyes of the brigands (and thus at the same time to those of the reader) is now drawn, like the landscape in the background, in a series of single pictures strung together to produce gradually a complete visual impression. It is a method not unlike camera-shot sequences in modern films. Together with the brigands we look down from above and observe in succession a heavily laden, unmanned ship, on the beach before it upturned tables and the remains of a sumptuous feast, and strewn between these the bodies of men just slain, some of the limbs still twitching. We go down to the beach with the brigands and see there – in a 'close-up' – a beautiful girl sitting on a rock and looking sadly (the brigands and we ourselves now follow her eyes) at the handsome young man who lies before her on the ground, wounded.

In the same way as he leads us step by step into the middle of his opening tableau without any kind of introduction, Heliodorus does not inform us until several scenes later that the couple on the beach are Chariclea and Theagenes (1.8). And only at the end of the first half of the novel, after five of ten books, are we finally furnished with all the information necessary for solving the mystery of the opening scene. It would scarcely be possible here to offer even just a rough outline of how, in the first five books of the *Aethiopica*, the events leading up to the brigands' appearance at the beginning are revealed in various flashbacks, while at the same time the story of the ensuing events is continued; how the author on the one hand further complicates the priest Calasiris' inserted account of the lovers' previous experiences by inserting into this other tales ('story within a story within a story'), and on the other hand intersperses it with remarks made by Cnemon, the man listening to the priest, so that it all takes on the character of a lively dialogue scene; how Cnemon himself becomes the central figure of a subplot which is related partly by the author, partly through the mouth of Cnemon; and, finally, how during the accounts given by Calasiris and Cnemon the main story, which even interrupts these tales, not only progresses steadily, but also provides new material for the development of the plot. Understandably we must confine ourselves here to a linear rendering of the most important events in the novel.

Chariclea, daughter of the Ethiopian king Hydaspes and his

queen Persinna, is exposed as a baby with one or two tokens of identification and grows up in Greece; the Egyptian Calasiris, whom Persinna sends to search for the child, finds her in Delphi, where Chariclea also meets Theagenes and their love begins. All three set out for Ethiopia but are captured at sea by pirates; the ship is driven by a storm into the Heracleotic mouth of the Nile, where two of the pirates, both of whom have fallen in love with Chariclea, start a fight which ends with all the pirates killing each other, this being the reason for the scene of devastation with which the novel opens. Calasiris is able to flee at this point, while the young couple fall into the hands of brigands. After more dangerous adventures with the brigands and another of their prisoners, the Athenian Cnemon (who has his own story to tell, having experienced something of the same type as the Phaedra tragedy), Chariclea and Theagenes are separated for a while; the girl meets with Calasiris again and is reunited with her beloved in Memphis, the priest's home. This all takes us into book 7, where the author now finally supplies the histories behind the various threads of the plot, one after the other; Cnemon having left the story for good in book 6 and the complicated family history of Calasiris having been unravelled – partly in flashbacks, partly as on-going events – the death of the priest now brings us to the point from which the Chariclea/ Theagenes story can be continued until the end of the novel in a single-thread line of action.

The most important events before the girl's return to her Ethiopian parents are quickly told. In Memphis the couple soon find themselves in trouble because Theagenes steadfastly resists all the advances made by the enamoured Arsace, wife of the Persian satrap (motifs from this episode were used for the libretto of Verdi's *Aida*); in this perilous situation the lovers' lives are saved at the last minute when the satrap, who is away fighting against the Ethiopians, but has been told of his wife's activities, sends for Chariclea and Theagenes. On their way to him the two are seized by Ethiopian reconnoitrers and taken to Hydaspes; after the besieged town of Syene has fallen to the Ethiopians – its capture is described at length in book 9 – the lovers seem doomed to be sacrificed to the gods during the victory celebrations. As in Xenophon of Ephesus (see above, p. 6), the parents' recognition of their child is delayed by a series of scenes which create additional suspense and tension. These include a trial by ordeal which proves the lovers both still to be chaste and pure, and heroic single combats between a now surprisingly animated Theagenes and first a raging bull, then an Ethiopian Samson – two wrestling-matches which clearly take up and modulate the idealistic novel's motif of the hero's military exploits. The work ends with the marriage of Theagenes and Chariclea and their ordination as priest and priestess of the deities Sun and Moon.

The technique used in the first half of the *Aethiopica*, where the plot is developed in flashbacks that provide the hitherto missing details, is very closely connected to a device which is used by Achilles Tatius in a similar fashion. As we have seen, the latter occasionally creates added suspense by having events related through the mouth of the first-person narrator only, who is himself directly involved and whose vision is therefore restricted. Heliodorus achieves in some episodes of his third-person narrative a comparable effect by temporarily relinquishing his position as omniscient author. For example, towards the end of the first book we (and Theagenes) are led to believe that Chariclea has been put to the sword by the marsh brigands' leader, the account of the deed being given from the point of view of the murderer; only at the beginning of book 2 do we (and Theagenes) learn that he was in fact mistaken in the identity of his victim (1.30 ff.). The refinement of narrative technique first tangible for us in, apart from the comic-realistic novels, Achilles Tatius is thus carried to perfection by Heliodorus. He also displays a mastery previously unattained in the idealistic novel in the realistic presentation of characters and objects. Of the countless narrative subtleties he uses to make fictional happenings seem authentic, one example must suffice here: never losing sight of the fact that Chariclea and Theagenes meet for the most part non-Greeks, Heliodorus consistently allows for the ensuing language problems (as in 1.3.4; 2.18 and elsewhere). Finally, the author's virtuosity in his command of the literary language cultivated by exponents of the Second Sophistic – a brilliance which he by no means reserves merely for the obligatory displays of rhetoric – can also only be hinted at here. His periods, laden with participle constructions and their word order frequently unorthodox, are often unfathomable, so that even his ancient readers will perhaps have had some difficulty with his Greek.

Alongside these projected improvements on Achilles Tatius and Longus as regards narrative technique, there is another step taken by the author of the *Aethiopica* – this time in connection with the content – which appears at first glance to be a relapse rather than an advance. I mean the revival of motifs typical of the older idealistic novels and, accompanying this, the particularly striking absence of the sexual psychology developed by his two 'rival' Neosophist novelists. However, Heliodorus makes one vital deviation from the pattern of events used in the earlier novels, for example in Xenophon of Ephesus' *Ephesiaca*, and it is a deviation which shows that he too was endeavouring to add a new intellectual dimension to the conventional material. His lovers do not return at the end of the novel to the Greek-speaking world whence they had started out on their adventures. Instead they spend the rest of their now blissful lives in a far-off land. This is localized nominally as a historically tangible reality – we are supposed to think of an age when the Persians still ruled over Egypt (fifth/fourth century BC) – but it is quite clearly to be understood as a political utopia. Heliodorus' Ethiopians are governed by an ideal ruler who has an open ear for the Neopythagorean and Neoplatonic wisdom of his priests, the gymnosophists. The citizens represent a society of perfect men and women; their noble humanitarian ethos comes fully to the fore after Chariclea, who was to have been sacrificed in their victory celebrations, is recognized by her parents: the people decide to offer their gods no more human sacrifices. With this, Heliodorus, who in the last lines of the novel names himself as a Phoenician from Emesa and priest of Helius, the highest Ethiopian deity, creates as setting for the traditional idealistic myth of salvation an additional fictional world, one of a visionary nature. The most probably earlier, 'earthly' model in Longus' idyllic pastoral environment is thus contrasted with a religious, philosophical realm.

The mention of the author's person brings us to the question of date for his work. Heliodorus seems to have known Philostratus' *Life of Apollonius of Tyana* (see above, pp. 18–19) and he talks of Persian armoured cavalry (9.14 f.), giving, however, a description of the mounted *cataphractarii* seen in Alexander Severus' campaign of 232–233; worship of the sun-god, which occurs in the novel, was declared an official cult under the Severan emperors. These considerations make it seem very likely that the *Aethiopica* was written in the second quarter of the third century, not very long after the other two fully extant Neosophist prose narratives. Some Heliodorus scholars are, however, firmly convinced that the *Aethiopica* was not written until the second half of the fourth century at the earliest. The theory is based on two orations of Emperor Julian in praise of Constantius II; these describe the siege of the Mesopotamian city of Nisibis by Sapor II in the year 350 (*or.* 1.27.B ff.; 2.63.C ff.). Julian's account, in particular the details given of a specific form of siege-craft, bears a striking resemblance to Heliodorus' depiction of the siege of Syene (book 9), and there can be no doubt that the one report is derived from the other. The first thought that comes to mind is, obviously, that the novelist modelled his account on the emperor's historical report. However, Tibor Szepessy's careful comparison of Julian's version with other ancient reports of the siege of Nisibis has shown that one particularly novel-like feature of the emperor's account – one which corresponds to a passage in the *Aethiopica* – represents a deviation from all other parallel historical accounts of the siege. Both Heliodorus and Julian describe how a lake is dug out around Syene so that the besieged city can be reached by boat. There is therefore nothing to contradict what has often been suggested: Emperor Julian, whom we know to have read idealistic novels (see above, p. 37), used the *Aethiopica* for the composition of his oration. We may thus continue to date the novel to the second quarter of the third century.

Those in favour of a later dating also like to argue that the fifth-century church historian Socrates Scholasticus cites the *Aethiopica* as an early work of Heliodorus, who then went on to become bishop of Tricca in Thessaly and introduced celibacy there. Another church historian writing much later (around 1320), Nicephorus Callistus, tells us that Heliodorus was called upon by a synod either to burn his novel or resign his ecclesiastical office. This information does not necessarily lend any degree of plausibility to the earlier assertions, which themselves quite definitely cannot be considered substantiated by the breath of Christian spirit allegedly perceptible in the humaneness shown by Heliodorus' Ethiopian gymnosophists. In any case, according to the *Suda*, Achilles Tatius too acquired the rank of bishop and yet this was an author who, as we have seen, displayed a lively interest in patterns of sexual behaviour and who could hardly be said to have expressed sentiments likely to earn him a mitre. There is only one tenable explanation for the ecclesiastical honours bestowed on Heliodorus and Achilles Tatius. At the end of the second and beginning of the third century, when a number of authors educated in the spirit of Neosophistic classicism attempted to reform the style and content of a genre created in late Hellenistic times, that is of the idealistic novel, early Christian novels, which themselves had derived from the same root in the second century (see above, pp. 22 ff.), already enjoyed considerable popularity. This was so great that the new pagan works, which made relatively high literary demands of their audience, could not compete for very long with the Christian light fiction and its compensatory value for contemporary readers. Apparently, however, the refined narrative skill shown in the later idealistic novels still found sufficient appreciation for their two most prominent authors simply to be Christianized *ex post facto*.

Heliodorus' work marks not only the zenith of the genre in respect of form, but also the end of the 'ancient novel' as such. The liberal ideological allowances made for the pagan content of the *Aethiopica* and of other Greek prose narratives are the principal explanation for the influence they had in Byzantium, where they continued to be copied and, in the twelfth century, were even imitated. In western Europe, however, this branch of Greek and Roman literature was not to become known until the Renaissance. Italian humanists then rediscovered the Latin texts of Petronius and Apuleius, and the surviving Greek literature was brought from eastern Mediterranean countries by Greek emigrants fleeing Turkish rule or by travellers who visited libraries there. Within the bounds of an introduction such as this, any attempt to follow the trail of the ancient novel from the sixteenth century onwards could offer no more than the usual, ultimately useless list of authors, titles and dates. A number of preliminary studies on the subject already exist, but it is a field which has yet to be fully explored. However, that is a task I must leave to another.

SELECT BIBLIOGRAPHY

TEXTS

This bibliography is divided into texts and secondary works. The secondary works are divided up by subject and works are listed chronologically.

COLLECTED ENGLISH TRANSLATIONS: B. P. Reardon (ed.), *Collected Ancient Greek Novels* (Berkeley/Los Angeles/London, 1989).

EDITIONS OF FRAGMENTS: B. Lavagnini (ed.), *Eroticorum Graecorum fragmenta papyracea* (Leipzig, 1922); F. Zimmermann (ed.), *Griechische Roman-Papyri und verwandte Texte* (Heidelberg, 1936); R. Kussl, *Papyrusfragmente griechischer Romane: Ausgewählte Untersuchungen* (Tübingen, 1991); S. Stephens/J. J. Winkler (eds), *Ancient Greek Novels: The Fragments* (Princeton, 1994).

ACHILLES TATIUS, *Leucippe and Clitophon*: edn + comm. E. Vilborg (Stockholm/Göteborg, 1955–62); edn + English trans. S. Gaselee, Loeb Classical Library (London/Cambridge, Mass., 1917); edn + French trans. J.-Ph. Garnaud, Collection Budé (Paris, 1991); German trans. + comm. K. Plepelits (Stuttgart, 1980) [excellent introduction]; English trans. J. J. Winkler in Reardon (*op. cit.*).

ANTONIUS DIOGENES, *The Wonders Beyond Thule*: edn + Latin trans. of summary M. Fusillo/A. Schottus (Palermo, 1990); English trans. of summary G. N. Sandy in Reardon (*op. cit.*); edn + English trans. of summary and fragments Stephens/Winkler (*op. cit.*).

APOCRYPHAL ACTS OF THE APOSTLES: edn R. Lipsius/M. Bonnet (Leipzig, 1891–1903; repr. Darmstadt, 1959); English trans. W. Wright (London, 1871); M. R. James (Oxford, [6]1955); German trans. E. Hennecke/W. Schneemelcher (Tübingen, [5]1989), trans. into English by R. M. Wilson (Cambridge, 1992).

APULEIUS, *Metamorphoses*: edn R. Helm, Bibliotheca Teubneriana (Leipzig, [3]1931; repr. 1992); edn + French trans. D. S. Robertson/P. Vallette, Collection Budé (Paris, [2]1956); edn +.English trans. J. A. Hanson, Loeb Classical Library (Cambridge, Mass./London, 1989); comm. on book 1

M. Molt (doct. diss. University of Groningen, 1938); A. Scobie (Meisenheim, 1975); on book 2 B. J. de Jonge (doct. diss. University of Groningen, 1941); on book 3 R. Th. van der Paardt (Amsterdam, 1971); on 4.1–27 B. L. Hijmans *et al.* (Groningen, 1977); on *Cupid and Psyche* P. Grimal (Paris, 1963); E. J. Kenney (Cambridge, 1990); on book 5 J. M. H. Fernhout (doct. diss. University of Groningen, 1949); on 6.25–32 and book 7 B. L. Hijmans *et al.* (Groningen, 1981); on book 8 B. L. Hijmans *et al.* (Groningen, 1985); on book 9 B. L. Hijmans *et al.* (Groningen, 1994); on 10.1–22 M. Zimmerman-de Graaf (doct. diss. University of Groningen, 1992); on book 11 J.-C. Fredouille (Paris, 1975); J. G. Griffiths (Leiden, 1975).

Ass Romance: edn of PSEUDO-LUCIAN, *Onos* (= epitome) M. D. Macleod, *Luciani Opera*, vol. ii, Oxford Classical Texts (Oxford, 1974); edn + English trans. M. D. Macleod, *Lucian*, vol. viii, Loeb Classical Library (London/Cambridge, Mass., 1967); English trans. J. P. Sullivan in Reardon (*op. cit.*).

Calligone: edn + English trans. of fragments Stephens/Winkler (*op. cit.*); English trans. B. P. Reardon in Reardon (*op. cit.*).

CHARITON, *Callirhoe*: edn W. E. Blake (Oxford, 1938); edn + French trans. G. Molinié, Collection Budé (Paris, ²1989); German trans. + comm. K. Plepelits (Stuttgart, 1976) [excellent introduction]; English trans. B. P. Reardon in Reardon (*op. cit.*).

Chione: edn + English trans. of fragments Stephens/Winkler (*op. cit.*); English trans. B. P. Reardon in Reardon (*op. cit.*).

DARES PHRYGIUS: edn F. Meister, Bibliotheca Teubneriana (Leipzig, 1873; repr. 1991); English trans. R. M. Frazer (Bloomington/London, 1966).

DICTYS CRETENSIS: edn W. Eisenhut, Bibliotheca Teubneriana (Leipzig, ²1973); English trans. R. M. Frazer (Bloomington/London, 1966); H. J. Marblestone (unpubl. doct. diss. Brandeis University, 1970).

EUHEMERUS OF MESSENE: edn M. Winiarczyk, Bibliotheca Teubneriana (Leipzig, 1991); edn + English trans. C. H. Oldfather, *Diodorus of Sicily*, vol. iii, Loeb Classical Library (London/Cambridge, Mass., 1939).

HELIODORUS, *Aethiopica*: edn A. Colonna (Roma, 1938; repr. Torino, 1987); edn + French trans. R. M. Rattenbury/T. W. Lumb/J. Maillon, Collection Budé (Paris, ²1960); English trans. J. R. Morgan in Reardon (*op. cit.*).

Herpyllis: edn + German trans. of fragments Kussl (*op. cit.*); edn + English trans. Stephens/Winkler (*op. cit.*); English trans. B. P. Reardon in Reardon (*op. cit.*).

Historia Apollonii regis Tyri: edn G. A. A. Kortekaas (Groningen, 1984); G. Schmeling, Bibliotheca Teubneriana (Leipzig, 1988); edn + English trans. E. Archibald (Cambridge, 1991); English trans. Z. Pavlovskis (Lawrence, Kan., 1978).

IAMBLICHUS, *Babyloniaca*: edn of summary and fragments E. Habrich,

Bibliotheca Teubneriana (Leipzig, 1960); edn + English trans. of summary and fragments Stephens/Winkler (*op. cit.*); English trans. of summary G. N. Sandy in Reardon (*op. cit.*).

IAMBULUS: edn + English trans. of Diod. 2.55–60 C. H. Oldfather, *Diodorus of Sicily*, vol. ii, Loeb Classical Library (London/Cambridge, Mass., 1935).

Iolaus: edn + English trans. of fragments P. Parsons, *The Oxyrhynchus Papyri* 42 (1974), 34–41; Stephens/Winkler (*op. cit.*); English trans. G. N. Sandy in Reardon (*op. cit.*).

JULIUS VALERIUS, *Res gestae Alexandri Macedonis*: edn M. Rosellini, Bibliotheca Teubneriana (Stuttgart/Leipzig, 1993).

Letters of Aischines: edn + French trans. V. Martin/G. Budé, Collection Budé (Paris, 1952).

Letters of Chion: edn + English trans. I. Düring (Göteborg, 1951; repr. New York, 1979).

Letters of Euripides: edn + German trans. H.-U. Gösswein (Meisenheim, 1975).

Letters of Hippocrates: edn + modern Greek trans. Th. Sakalis (Ioannina, 1989); edn + English trans. W. D. Smith (Leiden, 1990).

Letters of Plato: edn + English trans. R. G. Bury, *Plato*, vol. ix, Loeb Classical Library (London/Cambridge, Mass., 1929).

Letters of Socrates and the Socratics: edn + English trans. R. Malherbe, *The Cynic Epistles* (Missoula, Mont., 1977), 217–307.

Letters of Themistocles: edn G. Cortassa (Padova, 1990); edn + English trans. A. Doenges (New York, 1981).

Life of Aesop: edn B. E. Perry, *Aesopica* (Urbana, Ill., 1952; repr. New York, 1980); edn + modern Greek trans. M. Papathomopoulos (Ioannina, 1990); English trans. L. W. Daly (New York/London, 1961).

LOLLIANUS, *Phoenicica*: edn of fragments A. Henrichs (Bonn, 1972); edn + English trans. Stephens/Winkler (*op. cit.*); English trans. G. N. Sandy in Reardon (*op. cit.*).

LONGUS, *Daphnis and Chloe*: edn M. D. Reeve, Bibliotheca Teubneriana (Leipzig, ³1994); edn + English trans. G. Thornley/J. M. Edmonds, Loeb Classical Library (London/Cambridge, Mass., 1916); W. D. Lowe (New York, 1979); edn + French trans. G. Dalmeyda, Collection Budé (Paris, ²1960); J.-R. Vieillefond, Collection Budé (Paris, 1987); edn + German trans. O. Schönberger (Berlin, ³1980); English trans. C. Gill in Reardon (*op. cit.*).

LUCIAN, *True Stories*: edn M. D. Macleod, *Luciani Opera*, vol. i, Oxford Classical Texts (Oxford, 1972); edn + English trans. A. M. Harmon, *Lucian*, vol. i, Loeb Classical Library (London/Cambridge, Mass., 1913); English trans. B. P. Reardon in Reardon (*op. cit.*).

Ninus: edn + German trans. of fragments Kussl (*op. cit.*); edn + English trans. Stephens/Winkler (*op. cit.*); English trans. G. N. Sandy in Reardon (*op. cit.*).

Parthenope: edn + English trans. of fragments Stephens/Winkler (*op. cit.*).

PETRONIUS, *Satyrica*: edn + German trans. K. Müller/W. Ehlers, Sammlung Tusculum (München, ³1983); edn + English trans. M. Heseltine, Loeb Classical Library (Cambridge, Mass./London, ²1960); English trans. J. P. Sullivan, Penguin Classics (Harmondsworth, ²1969); comm. on *Cena* L. Friedländer (Leipzig, ²1906; repr. Amsterdam, 1960); M. S. Smith (Oxford, 1975); comm. on inserted poems H. Stubbe (Leipzig, 1933); E. Courtney (Atlanta, 1991); comm. on 'Bellum Civile' G. Guido (Bologna, 1976); comm. on inserted novellas P. Fedeli/ R. Dimundo (Roma, 1988).

PHILOSTRATUS, *Life of Apollonius of Tyana*: edn K. L. Kayser, Bibliotheca Teubneriana (Leipzig, 1870); edn + English trans. F. C. Conybeare, Loeb Classical Library (London/Cambridge, Mass., 1912).

PSEUDO-CALLISTHENES, *Alexander Romance*: edn of version A W. Kroll (Berlin, 1926); English trans. of version A K. Dowden in Reardon (*op. cit.*); R. Stoneman, Penguin Classics (Harmondsworth, 1991); edn + German trans. of MS. L. H. van Thiel (Darmstadt, 1983).

Pseudo-Clementines: edn B. Rehm/F. Paschke (Berlin, 1965–9).

Sesonchosis: edn + English trans. of fragments Stephens/Winkler (*op. cit.*); English trans. G. N. Sandy in Reardon (*op. cit.*).

XENOPHON OF ATHENS, *Cyropaedia*: edn + English trans. W. Miller, Loeb Classical Library (London/Cambridge, Mass., 1914); edn + French trans. M. Bizos/E. Delebecque, Collection Budé (Paris, 1972–8).

XENOPHON OF EPHESUS, *Ephesiaca*: edn A. D. Papanikolaou, Bibliotheca Teubneriana (Leipzig, 1973); edn + French trans. G. Dalmeyda, Collection Budé (Paris, 1926); English trans. G. Anderson in Reardon (*op. cit.*).

SECONDARY WORKS

Annotated bibliographies

L'Année philologique (Paris, 1924 ff.), see under 'Auteurs et textes' (for individual authors and 'Narrativa') and 'Histoire littéraire: Littérature narrative . . .'.

O. Mazal, 'Der griechische und byzantinische Roman in der Forschung von 1945–1960', *Jahrbuch der Österreichischen Byzantinischen Gesellschaft* 11/12 (1962/63), 9–55; 13 (1964), 29–86; 14 (1965), 83–124.

G. Schmeling (ed.), *The Petronian Society Newsletter* (Gainesville, Fla., 1970 ff.).

C. C. Schlam, 'The Scholarship on Apuleius since 1938', *Classical World* 64 (1970/71), 285–309; also in: *The Classical World Bibliography of Roman Drama and Poetry and Ancient Fiction* (New York/London, 1978).

G. N. Sandy, 'Recent Scholarship on the Prose Fiction of Classical Antiquity', *Classical World* 67 (1974), 321–59; also in: *The Classical*

World Bibliography of Roman Drama and Poetry and Ancient Fiction (New York/London, 1978).

G. L. Schmeling/J. H. Stuckey, *A Bibliography of Petronius* (Leiden, 1977).

M. S. Smith, 'A Bibliography of Petronius (1945–1982)', *Aufstieg und Niedergang der Römischen Welt* ii. 32.3 (1985), 1624–65.

E. L. Bowie/S. J. Harrison, 'The Romance of the Novel', *Journal of Roman Studies* 83 (1993) 159–78.

General discussions and collected papers

Ancient prose fiction: general

A. Heiserman, *The Novel before the Novel: Essays and Discussions about the Beginnings of Prose Fiction in the West* (Chicago/London, 1977).

B. P. Reardon (ed.), *Erotica antiqua: Acta of the International Conference on the Ancient Novel* (Bangor, 1977).

T. Hägg, *The Novel in Antiquity* (Oxford, 1983).

H. Hofmann (ed.), *Groningen Colloquia on the Novel* (Groningen, 1988 ff.).

H. Kuch (ed.), *Der antike Roman: Untersuchungen zur literarischen Kommunikation und Gattungsgeschichte* (Berlin, 1989).

J. Tatum/G. M. Vernazza (eds), *The Ancient Novel: Classical Paradigms and Modern Perspectives. Proceedings of the International Conference* (Hanover, NH, 1990).

J. Tatum (ed.), *The Search for the Ancient Novel* (Baltimore/London, 1994).

The Greek novel

B. P. Reardon, *Courants littéraires grecs des IIe et IIIe siècles après J.-C.* (Paris, 1971), 309–405.

C. W. Müller, 'Der griechische Roman', in E. Vogt (ed.), *Griechische Literatur*, Neues Handbuch der Literaturwissenschaft, vol. ii (Wiesbaden, 1981), 377–412.

H. Gärtner (ed.), *Beiträge zum griechischen Liebesroman* (Hildesheim/ Zürich/New York, 1984).

E. L. Bowie, 'The Greek Novel', in *The Cambridge History of Classical Literature*, vol. i (Cambridge, 1985), 683–99.

R. Beaton (ed.), *The Greek Novel AD 1–1985* (London/New York/Sydney, 1988).

M.-F. Baslez/P. Hoffmann/M. Trédé (eds), *Le monde du roman grec: Actes du Colloque Internationale* (Paris, 1992).

J. R. Morgan/R. Stoneman (eds), *Greek Fiction: The Greek Novel in Context* (London/New York, 1994).

The Roman novel

P. G. Walsh, *The Roman Novel: The 'Satyricon' of Petronius and the 'Metamorphoses' of Apuleius* (Cambridge, 1970).

The genre: origins and definition

E. Rohde, *Der griechische Roman und seine Vorläufer* (Leipzig, [1876] ³1914; repr. Darmstadt, 1974).

E. Schwartz, *Fünf Vorträge über den griechischen Roman* (Berlin, 1896; repr. 1943).

K. Kerényi, *Die griechisch-orientalische Romanliteratur in religionsgeschichtlicher Beleuchtung* (Tübingen, 1927; repr. Darmstadt, 1973).

F. Altheim, 'Roman und Dekadenz', in Altheim, *Literatur und Gesellschaft im ausgehenden Altertum*, vol. i (Halle, 1948), 13–47 (repr. as book, Tübingen, 1951).

G. Giangrande, 'On the Origins of the Greek Romance: The Birth of a Literary Form', *Eranos* 60 (1962), 132–59; also in Gärtner, *Beiträge* (see under 'The Greek novel', p. 110), 125–52.

R. Merkelbach, *Roman und Mysterium in der Antike* (München/Berlin, 1962).

F. Wehrli, 'Einheit und Vorgeschichte der griechisch-römischen Romanliteratur', *Museum Helveticum* 22 (1964), 133–54; also in Gärtner, *Beiträge* (see under 'The Greek novel', p. 110), 161–82.

B. E. Perry, *The Ancient Romances: A Literary-Historical Account of their Origins* (Berkeley/Los Angeles, 1967).

B. P. Reardon, 'The Greek Novel', *Phoenix* 23 (1969), 291–309; also in Gärtner, *Beiträge* (see under 'The Greek novel', p. 110), 218–36.

G. Anderson, *Ancient Fiction: The Novel in the Graeco-Roman World* (London/Sydney, 1984).

B. P. Reardon, *The Form of Greek Romance* (Princeton, 1991).

N. Holzberg, 'Ktesias von Knidos und der griechische Roman', *Würzburger Jahrbücher für die Altertumswissenschaft* 19 (1993), 79–84.

J. R. Morgan, 'Make-Believe and Make Believe: The Fictionality of the Greek Novels', in C. Gill/T. P. Wiseman (eds), *Lies and Fiction in the Ancient World* (Exeter, 1993), 175–229.

D. L. Selden, 'Genre of Genre', in Tatum, *The Search* (see under 'Ancient prose fiction', p. 110), 39–64.

J. J. Winkler, 'The Invention of Romance', in Tatum, *The Search* (see under 'Ancient prose fiction', p. 110), 23–38.

Specific aspects: narrative technique, motifs, readership

T. Hägg, *Narrative Technique in Ancient Greek Romances: Studies of Chariton, Xenophon Ephesius and Achilles Tatius* (Stockholm, 1971).

THE ANCIENT NOVEL

B. Effe, 'Entstehung und Funktion "personaler" Erzählweisen in der Erzählliteratur der Antike', *Poetica* 7 (1975), 135–57.

G. Anderson, *Eros Sophistes: Ancient Novelists at Play* (Chico, Calif., 1982).

B. Effe, 'Der griechische Liebesroman und die Homoerotik', *Philologus* 131 (1987), 95–108.

C. Ruiz Montero, *La estructura de la novela griega* (Salamanca, 1988).

B. Wesseling, 'The Audience of the Ancient Novels', *Groningen Colloquia on the Novel* 1 (1988), 67–79.

M. Fusillo, *Il romanzo greco: Polifonia ed Eros* (Venezia, 1989); French trans. *Naissance du roman* (Paris, 1991).

P. Liviabella Furiani/A. M. Scarcella (eds), *Piccolo mondo antico: appunti sulle donne, gli amori, i costumi, il mondo reale nel romanzo antico* (Napoli, 1989).

B. Egger, *Constructing the Feminine: Women in the Greek Novels* (unpubl. doct. diss. University of California, 1990).

S. Wiersma, 'The Ancient Greek Novel and Its Heroines: A Female Paradox', *Mnemosyne* 63 (1990), 109–123.

A. Billault, *La création romanesque dans la littérature grecque à l'époque impériale* (Paris, 1991).

H. Montague, 'Sweet and Pleasant Passion: Female and Male Fantasy in Ancient Romance Novels', in A. Richlin (ed.), *Pornography and Representation in Greece and Rome* (New York/Oxford, 1992), 231–49.

E. Bowie, 'The Readership of Greek Novels in the Ancient World', in Tatum, *The Search* (see under 'Ancient prose fiction', p. 110), 435–59.

F. Létoublon, *Les lieux communs du roman: stéréotypes grecs d'aventure et d'amour* (Leiden, 1993).

T. Hägg, 'Orality, Literacy, and the "Readership" of the Early Greek Novel', in R. Eriksen (ed.), *Contexts of Pre-Novel Narrative: The European Tradition* (Berlin/New York, 1994), 47–81.

D. Konstan, *Sexual Symmetry: Love in the Ancient Novel and Related Genres* (Princeton, 1994).

J. R. Morgan, 'The Greek Novel: Towards a Sociology of Production and Reception', in A. Powell (ed.), *The Greek World* (London, 1995).

S. A. Stephens, 'Who Read Ancient Novels?', in Tatum, *The Search* (see under 'Ancient prose fiction', p. 110), 405–18.

Achilles Tatius

D. B. Durham, 'Parody in Achilles Tatius', *Classical Philology* 33 (1938), 1–19.

D. Sedelmeier, 'Studien zu Achilleus Tatios', *Wiener Studien* 72 (1959), 113–43; also in Gärtner, *Beiträge* (see under 'The Greek novel', p. 110), 330–60.

S. Bartsch, *Decoding the Ancient Novel: The Reader and the Role of*

Description in Heliodorus and Achilles Tatius (Princeton, 1989).
G. Most, 'The Stranger's Stratagem: Self-Disclosure and Self-Sufficiency in Greek Culture', *Journal of Hellenic Studies* 109 (1989), 114–33.
B. P. Reardon, 'Achilles Tatius and Ego-Narrative', in Morgan/Stoneman, *Greek Fiction* (see under 'The Greek novel', p. 110), 80–96.

Antonius Diogenes

K. Reyhl, *Antonios Diogenes: Untersuchungen zu den Roman-Fragmenten der 'Wunder jenseits von Thule' und zu den 'Wahren Geschichten' des Lukian* (doct. diss. University of Tübingen, 1969).
A. Borgogno, 'Sulla stuttura degli *Apista* di Antonio Diogene', *Prometheus* 1 (1975), 49–64.
W. Fauth, 'Astraios und Zamolxis: Über Spuren pythagoreischer Aretalogie im Thule-Roman des Antonius Diogenes', *Hermes* 106 (1978), 220–41.
W. Fauth, 'Zur kompositorischen Anlage und zur Typik der Apista des Antonius Diogenes', *Würzburger Jahrbücher für die Altertumswissenschaft* 4 (1978), 57–68.
A. Borgogno, 'Antonio Diogene e le trame dei romanzi greci', *Prometheus* 5 (1979), 137–56.
J. R. Morgan, 'Lucian's *True Histories* and the *Wonders Beyond Thule* of Antonius Diogenes', *Classical Quarterly* 35 (1985), 475–90.
S. Swain, 'Antonius Diogenes and Lucian', *Liverpool Classical Monthly* 17 (1992), 74–6.
J. Romm, 'Novels Beyond Thule: Antonius Diogenes, Rabelais, Cervantes', in Tatum, *The Search* (see under 'Ancient prose fiction', p. 110), 101–16.

Apocryphal Acts of the Apostles

R. Söder, *Die apokryphen Apostelgeschichten und die romanhafte Literatur der Antike* (Stuttgart, 1932).
E. Plümacher, 'Apokryphe Apostelakten', *Pauly-Wissowa Suppl.* xv (1978), 11–70.
F. Bovon *et al.*, *Les actes apocryphes des apôtres* (Genève, 1981).
D. R. Edwards, *Acts of the Apostles and Chariton's Chaereas and Callirhoe: A Literary and Sociohistorical Study* (unpubl. doct. diss. Boston University, 1987).
D. R. Edwards, 'The New Testament and the Ancient Romance: A Survey of Recent Research', *Petronian Society Newsletter* 17 (1987), 9–14.
R. I. Pervo, *Profit with Delight: The Literary Genre of the Acts of the Apostles* (Minneapolis, 1987).
Aufstieg und Niedergang der Römischen Welt ii. 25.6 (1988), 4293 ff. [= 5 papers on the Apocryphal Acts].

THE ANCIENT NOVEL

J. Perkins, 'The Apocryphal Acts of Peter: A Roman à Thèse?', *Arethusa* 25 (1992), 445–55.

J. Perkins, 'The Social World of the Acts of Peter', in Tatum, *The Search* (see under 'Ancient prose fiction', p. 110), 296–307.

R. I. Pervo, 'Early Christian Fiction', in Morgan/Stoneman, *Greek Fiction* (see under 'The Greek novel', p. 110), 239–54.

Apuleius, *Metamorphoses*

P. Junghanns, *Die Erzählungstechnik von Apuleius' Metamorphosen und ihrer Vorlage* (Leipzig, 1932).

G. Binder/R. Merkelbach (eds), *Amor und Psyche* (Darmstadt, 1968).

D. Fehling, *Amor und Psyche: Die Schöpfung des Apuleius und ihre Einwirkung auf das Märchen, eine Kritik der romantischen Märchentheorie* (Mainz, 1977).

B. L. Hijmans/R. Th. van der Paardt (eds), *Aspects of Apuleius' Golden Ass* (Groningen, 1978).

J. Tatum, *Apuleius and The Golden Ass* (Ithaca, N.Y./London, 1979).

B. L. Hijmans/V. Schmidt (eds), *Symposium Apuleianum Groninganum 1980* (Groningen, 1981).

F. Millar, 'The World of the *Golden Ass*', *Journal of Roman Studies* 71 (1981), 63–75.

R. Th. van der Paardt, 'The Unmasked "I": Apuleius *Met.* XI 27', *Mnemosyne* 34 (1981), 96–106.

K. Dowden, 'Apuleius and the Art of Narration', *Classical Quarterly* 32 (1982), 419–35.

K. Dowden, 'Psyche on the Rock', *Latomus* 41 (1982), 336–52.

P. Steinmetz, *Untersuchungen zur römischen Literatur des zweiten Jahrhunderts nach Christi Geburt* (Wiesbaden, 1982), 239–75.

C. Harrauer/F. Römer, 'Beobachtungen zum Metamorphosen-Prolog des Apuleius', *Mnemosyne* 38 (1985), 353–72.

J. J. Winkler, *Auctor & Actor: A Narratological Reading of Apuleius's The Golden Ass* (Berkeley/Los Angeles/London, 1985).

G. F. Gianotti, *'Romanzo' e ideologia: studi sulle Metamorfosi di Apuleio* (Napoli, 1986).

P. James, *Unity in Diversity: A Study of Apuleius' Metamorphoses with Particular Reference to the Narrator's Art of Transformation and the Metamorphosis Motif in the Tale of Cupid and Psyche* (Hildesheim/Zürich/New York, 1987).

N. Holzberg, 'Einführung', in E. Brandt/W. Ehlers (eds), *Apuleius: Der Goldene Esel* (München, ⁴1989), 549–74.

J. L. Penwill, '*Ambages reciprocae*: Reviewing Apuleius' Metamorphoses', *Ramus* 19 (1990), 1–25.

C. C. Schlam, *The Metamorphoses of Apuleius: On Making an Ass of Oneself* (Chapel Hill/London, 1992).

114

H. Hofmann, 'Parodie des Erzählens – Erzählen als Parodie: Der Goldene Esel des Apuleius', in W. Ax/R. F. Glei (eds), *Literaturparodie in Antike und Mittelalter* (Trier, 1993), 119–51.

A. Laird, 'Fiction, Bewitchment and Story Worlds: The Implications of Claims to Truth in Apuleius', in C. Gill/T. P. Wiseman (eds), *Lies and Fiction in the Ancient World* (Exeter, 1993), 147–74.

L. Callebat, 'Formes et modes d'expression dans les œuvres d'Apulée', *Aufstieg und Niedergang der Römischen Welt* ii. 34.2 (1994), 1600–64.

K. Dowden, 'The Roman Audience of *The Golden Ass*', in Tatum, *The Search* (see under 'Ancient prose fiction', p. 110), 419–34.

G. N. Sandy, 'Apuleius' "Metamorphoses" and the Ancient Novel', *Aufstieg und Niedergang der Römischen Welt* ii. 34.2 (1994), 1511–74.

W. S. Smith, 'Style and Character in "The Golden Ass": "Suddenly an Opposite Appearance"', *Aufstieg und Niedergang der Römischen Welt* ii. 34.2 (1994), 1575–99.

Ass Romance

P. Junghanns, *Die Erzählungstechnik* (see under 'Apuleius', p. 114).

A. Lesky, 'Apuleius von Madaura und Lukios von Patrai', *Hermes* 76 (1941), 43–74; also in Lesky, *Gesammelte Schriften* (Bern/München, 1966), 549–78.

H. van Thiel, *Der Eselsroman*, 2 vols (München, 1971–2).

G. Anderson, *Studies in Lucian's Comic Fiction* (Leiden, 1976), 34–67.

B. Effe, 'Der mißglückte Selbstmord des Aristomenes (Apul. Met. 1,14–17): Zur Romanparodie im griechischen Eselsroman', *Hermes* 104 (1976), 362–75.

J. A. Hall, *Lucian's Satire* (New York, 1981).

N. Holzberg, 'Apuleius und der Verfasser des griechischen Eselsromans', *Würzburger Jahrbücher für die Altertumswissenschaft* 10 (1984), 161–77.

R. Kussl, 'Die Metamorphosen des "Lukios von Patrai": Untersuchungen zu Phot. Bibl. 129', *Rheinisches Museum* 133 (1990), 379–88.

H. J. Mason, 'Greek and Latin Versions of the Ass-Story', *Aufstieg und Niedergang der Römischen Welt* ii. 34.2 (1994), 1665–707.

Chariton

B. E. Perry, 'Chariton and his Romance from a Literary-Historical Point of View', *American Journal of Philology* 51 (1930), 93–134; also in Gärtner, *Beiträge* (see under 'The Greek novel', p. 110), 237–78.

A. D. Papanikolaou, *Chariton-Studien: Untersuchungen zur Sprache und Chronologie der griechischen Romane* (Göttingen, 1973).

K. H. Gerschmann, *Chariton-Interpretationen* (doct. diss. University of Münster, 1974).

G. L. Schmeling, *Chariton* (New York, 1974).

C. W. Müller, 'Chariton von Aphrodisias und die Theorie des Romans in der Antike', *Antike und Abendland* 22 (1976), 115–36.

M. Laplace, 'Les légendes troyennes dans le "roman" de Chariton, *Chairéas et Callirhoé*', *Revue des Études Grecques* 93 (1980), 83–125.

B. P. Reardon, 'Theme, Structure and Narrative in Chariton', *Yale Classical Studies* 27 (1982), 1–27.

B. Egger, 'Looking at Chariton's Callirhoe', in Morgan/Stoneman, *Greek Fiction* (see under 'The Greek novel', p. 110), 31–48.

R. Hunter, 'History and Historicity in the Romance of Chariton', *Aufstieg und Niedergang der Römischen Welt* ii. 34.2 (1994), 1055–86.

C. Ruiz Montero, 'Chariton von Aphrodisias: Ein Überblick', *Aufstieg und Niedergang der Römischen Welt* ii. 34.2 (1994), 1006–54.

Chione

N. Marini, 'Osservazioni sul "Romanzo di Chione"', *Athenaeum* 80 (1993), 587–600.

Dares Phrygius and Dictys Cretensis

A. M. Milazzo, 'Achille e Polissena in Ditti Cretese: un romanzo nel romanzo?', *Le forme e la storia* 5 (1984), 3–24.

K. C. King, *Achilles: Paradigms of the War Hero from Homer to the Middle Ages* (Berkeley/Los Angeles/London, 1987), 138–43, 195–201.

W. Schetter, 'Beobachtungen zum Dares Latinus', *Hermes* 116 (1988), 94–109.

S. Timpanaro, 'Sulla composizione e la tecnica narrativa dell'Ephemeris di Ditti-Settimio', in *Filologia e forme letterarie*, vol. iv (Urbino, 1988), 169–215.

S. Merkle, *Die Ephemeris belli Troiani des Diktys von Kreta* (Frankfurt am Main/Bern/New York/Paris, 1989).

L. de Biasi, 'Ditti Cretese e Darete Frigio (concenni sul romanzo)', in I. Lana (ed.), *La storiografia latina del IV secolo D.C.* (Torino, 1990), 210–19.

A. Beschorner, *Untersuchungen zu Dares Phrygius* (Tübingen, 1992).

J. Dingel, 'Spätantike Troja-Romane', in I. Garner-Wallert (ed.), *Troia, Brücke zwischen Orient und Okzident* (Tübingen, 1992), 219–29.

S. Merkle, 'Telling the True Story of the Trojan War: The Eyewitness Account of Dictys of Crete', in Tatum, *The Search* (see under 'Ancient prose fiction', p. 110), 183–96.

Epistolary novels

A. Billault, 'Les lettres de Chion d'Héraclée', *Revue des Études Grecques* 90 (1977), 29–37.

J. L. Penwill, 'The Letters of Themistokles: An Epistolary Novel?', *Antichthon* 12 (1978), 83–103.

A. Doenges, *The Letters of Themistocles* (New York, 1981).

R. G. Ussher, 'Love Letter, Novel, Alciphron and "Chion"', *Hermathena* 143 (1987), 99–106.

D. Konstan/P. Mitsis, 'Chion of Heracleia: A Philosophical Novel in Letters', *Apeiron* 23 (1990), 257–79.

N. Holzberg (ed.), *Der griechische Briefroman: Gattungstypologie und Textanalyse* (Tübingen, 1994).

P. A. Rosenmeyer, 'The Epistolary Novel', in Morgan/Stoneman, *Greek Fiction* (see under 'The Greek novel', p. 110), 146–65.

Euhemerus of Messene and Iambulus

D. Winston, *Iambulus: A Literary Study in Greek Utopianism* (unpubl. doct. diss. Columbia University, 1956).

J. Ferguson, *Utopias of the Classical World* (Ithaca, NY, 1975).

M. Zumschlinge, *Euhemeros: Staatstheoretische und staatsutopische Motive* (doct. diss. University of Bonn, 1976).

R. Bichler, 'Zur historischen Beurteilung der griechischen Staatsutopie', *Grazer Beiträge* 11 (1984), 179–206.

W.-W. Ehlers, 'Mit dem Südwestmonsun nach Ceylon: Eine Interpretation der Iambul-Exzerpte Diodors', *Würzburger Jahrbücher für die Altertumswissenschaft* 11 (1985), 73–84.

B. Kytzler, 'Zum utopischen Roman der klassischen Antike', *Groningen Colloquia on the Novel* 1 (1988), 7–16.

H. Kuch, 'Funktionswandlungen des antiken Romans', in Kuch, *Der antike Roman* (see under 'Ancient prose fiction', p. 110), 52–81.

J. Romm, *The Edges of the Earth in Ancient Thought* (Princeton, 1992).

R. J. Müller, 'Überlegungen zur *Hiera Anagraphe* des Euhemeros von Messene', *Hermes* 121 (1993), 276–300.

Heliodorus

V. Hefti, *Zur Erzählungstechnik in Heliodors Aethiopica* (Wien, 1950).

T. Szepessy, 'Die Aithiopika des Heliodoros und der griechische sophistische Liebesroman', *Acta Antiqua Academiae Scientiarum Hungaricae* 5 (1957), 241–59; also in Gärtner, *Beiträge* (see under 'The Greek novel', p. 110), 432–50.

T. Szepessy, 'Die "Neudatierung" des Heliodoros und die Belagerung von Nisibis', in *Actes de la XIIe conférence internationale d'études classiques 'Eirene'* (Amsterdam, 1975), 279–87.

W. Bühler, 'Das Element des Visuellen in der Eingangsszene von Heliodors Aithiopika', *Wiener Studien* 10 (1976), 177–85.

J. R. Morgan, 'History, Romance and Realism in the Aithiopika of

Heliodoros', *Classical Antiquity* 1 (1982), 221–65.

G. N. Sandy, *Heliodorus* (Boston, 1982).

J. J. Winkler, 'The Mendacity of Kalasiris and the Narrative Strategy of Heliodoros' *Aithiopika*', *Yale Classical Studies* 27 (1982), 93–158.

M. Futre Pinheiro, *Estruturas técnico-narrativas nas Etiópicas de Heliodoro* (Lisbão, 1987).

S. Bartsch, *Decoding the Ancient Novel* (see under 'Achilles Tatius', p. 112).

J. R. Morgan, 'A Sense of the Ending: The Conclusion of Heliodoros' *Aithiopika*', *Transactions and Proceedings of the American Philological Association* 119 (1989), 299–320.

J. R. Morgan, 'The Story of Knemon in Heliodoros' *Aithiopika*', *Journal of Hellenic Studies* 109 (1989), 99–113.

M. Futre Pinheiro, 'Calasiris' Story and its Narrative Significance in Heliodorus' *Aethiopica*', *Groningen Colloquia on the Novel* 4 (1991), 69–83.

M. Futre Pinheiro, 'Fonctions du surnaturel dans les *Éthiopiques* d'Héliodore', *Bulletin de l'Association Guillaume Budé* (1991), 359–81.

J. R. Morgan, 'Reader and Audiences in the *Aithiopika* of Heliodoros', *Groningen Colloquia on the Novel* 4 (1991), 85–103.

M. Laplace, 'Les *Éthiopiques* d'Héliodore, ou la genèse d'un panégyrique de l'Amour', *Revue des Études Anciennes* 94 (1992), 199–230.

T. Paulsen, *Inszenierung des Schicksals: Tragödie und Komödie im Roman des Heliodor* (Trier, 1992).

J. R. Morgan, 'The *Aithiopika* of Heliodoros: Narrative as Riddle', in Morgan/Stoneman, *Greek Fiction* (see under 'The Greek novel', p. 110), 97–113.

Herpyllis

R. Kussl, *Papyrusfragmente* (see under 'Texts': 'Editions of fragments', p. 106), 103–140.

Historia Apollonii regis Tyri

E. Klebs, *Die Erzählung von Apollonius aus Tyrus. Eine geschichtliche Untersuchung über ihre lateinische Urform und ihre späteren Bearbeitungen* (Berlin, 1899).

I. Lana (ed.), *Studi su il romanzo di Apollonio re di Tiro* (Torino, 1975).

R. Ziegler, 'Die "Historia Apollonii Regis Tyri" und der Kaiserkult in Tarsos', *Chiron* 14 (1984), 219–34.

M. Mazza, 'Le avventure del romanzo nell'occidente latino: la *Historia Apollonii Regis Tyri*', *Le Trasformazioni della Cultura nella Tarda Antichità* 2 (1985), 597–645.

T. Szepessy, 'The Ancient Family Novel (A Typological Proposal)', *Acta Antiqua Academiae Scientiarum Hungaricae* 31 (1985–8), 357–65.

G. Schmeling, 'Manners and Morality in the "Historia Apollonii regis Tyri"', in Liviabella Furiani/Scarcella, *Piccolo mondo antico* (see under 'Specific aspects', p. 112), 197–215.

N. Holzberg, 'The *Historia Apollonii regis Tyri* and the *Odyssey*', *Groningen Colloquia on the Novel* 3 (1990), 91–101.

E. Archibald, *Apollonius of Tyre: Medieval and Renaissance Themes and Variations* (Cambridge, 1991).

G. A. A. Kortekaas, 'The *Historia Apollonii regis Tyri* and Ancient Astrology: A Possible Link between Apollonius and *katoche*', *Zeitschrift für Papyrologie und Epigraphik* 85 (1991), 71–85.

R. Kussl, *Papyrusfragmente* (see under 'Texts': 'Editions of fragments', p. 106), 141–59.

C. W. Müller, 'Der Romanheld als Rätsellöser in der Historia Apollonii regis Tyri', *Würzburger Jahrbücher für die Altertumswissenschaft* 17 (1991), 267–79.

A. Stramaglia, 'Prosimetria narrativa e "romanzo perduto": PTurner 8 (con discussione e riedizione di PSI 151 [Pack^2 2624] + PMil Vogliano 260)', *Zeitschrift für Papyrologie und Epigraphik* 92 (1992), 121–49.

D. Konstan, '*Apollonius, King of Tyre* and the Greek Novel', in Tatum, *The Search* (see under 'Ancient prose fiction', p. 110), 173–82.

Iamblichus

U. Schneider-Menzel, 'Jamblichos' "Babylonische Geschichten"', in F. Altheim, *Literatur und Gesellschaft im ausgehenden Altertum*, vol. i (Halle, 1948), 48–92.

R. Beck, 'Soteriology, the Mysteries, and the Ancient Novel: Iamblichus' *Babyloniaca* as a Test-Case', in U. Bianchi/M. J. Vermaseren (eds), *La soteriologia dei culti orientali nell'imperio Romano. Atti del Colloquio Internazionale* (Leiden, 1982), 527–40.

Iambulus

See under 'Euhemerus' of Messene', p. 117.

Iolaus

P. Parsons, 'A Greek Satyricon?', *Bulletin of the Institute of Classical Studies* 18 (1971), 53–68.

G. N. Sandy, 'New Pages of Greek Fiction', in Morgan/Stoneman, *Greek Fiction* (see under 'The Greek novel', p. 110), 130–45.

Letters of Aischines, etc.

See under 'Epistolary novels', p. 116.

THE ANCIENT NOVEL

Life of Aesop

A. La Penna, 'Il Romanzo di Esopo', *Athenaeum* 40 (1962), 264–314.

B. Holbek, 'Äsop', in *Enzyklopädie des Märchens* 1 (1977), 882–9.

F. R. Adrados, 'The "Life of Aesop" and the Origins of the Novel in Antiquity', *Quaderni Urbinati di Cultura Classica* 30 (1979), 93–112.

S. Jedrkiewicz, *Sapere e paradosso nell'antichità: Esopo e la favola* (Roma, 1989).

A. Patterson, *Fables of Power: Aesopian Writing and Political History* (Durham/London, 1991).

N. Holzberg (ed.), *Der Äsop-Roman: Motivgeschichte und Erzählstruktur* (Tübingen, 1992).

N. Holzberg, 'A Lesser Known "Picaresque" Novel of Greek Origin: The *Aesop Romance* and its Influence', *Groningen Colloquia on the Novel* 5 (1993), 1–16.

K. Hopkins, 'Novel Evidence for Roman Slavery', *Past & Present* 138 (1993), 3–27.

Lollianus

A. Henrichs, *Die Phoinikika des Lollianos* (Bonn, 1972).

G. N. Sandy, 'Notes on Lollianus' *Phoenicica*', *American Journal of Philology* 100 (1979), 367–76.

C. P. Jones, 'Apuleius' *Metamorphoses* and Lollianus' *Phoinikika*', *Phoenix* 34 (1979), 243–54.

J. Winkler, 'Lollianos and the Desperadoes', *Journal of Hellenic Studies* 100 (1980), 155–81.

J. N. O'Sullivan, 'Some Thoughts on Lollianus fr. B 1', *Zeitschrift für Papyrologie und Epigraphik* 50 (1983), 7–11.

G. N. Sandy, 'New Pages of Greek Fiction' (see under '*Iolaus*', p. 119).

Longus

G. Rohde, 'Longus und die Bukolik', *Rheinisches Museum* 86 (1937), 23–49; also in Gärtner, *Beiträge* (see under 'The Greek novel', p. 110), 361–87.

H. H. O. Chalk, 'Eros and the Lesbian Pastorals of Longos', *Journal of Hellenic Studies* 80 (1960), 32–51; also in Gärtner, *Beiträge* (see under 'The Greek novel', p. 110), 388–407.

M. C. Mittelstadt, 'Longus: Daphnis and Chloe and Roman Narrative Painting', *Latomus* 26 (1967), 752–61.

W. E. McCulloh, *Longus, Daphnis and Chloe* (New York, 1970).

M. C. Mittelstadt, 'Bucolic-Lyric Motifs and Dramatic Narrative in Longus' Daphnis and Chloe', *Rheinisches Museum* 133 (1970), 211–27.

M. C. Mittelstadt, 'Love, Eros and Poetic Art in Longus', in *Fons perennis:*

SELECT BIBLIOGRAPHY

Saggi critici di filologia classica raccolti in onore di Vittorio d'Agostino (Torino, 1971), 305–32.

W. E. Forehand, 'Symbolic Gardens in Longus' Daphnis and Chloe', *Eranos* 74 (1976), 103–12.

A. Geyer, 'Roman und Mysterienritual: Zum Problem eines Bezugs zum dionysischen Mysterienritual im Roman des Longos', *Würzburger Jahrbücher für die Altertumswissenschaft* 3 (1977), 179–96.

B. Effe, 'Longos: Zur Funktionsgeschichte der Bukolik in der römischen Kaiserzeit', *Hermes* 110 (1982), 65–84.

R. L. Hunter, *A Study of Daphnis and Chloe* (Cambridge, 1983).

T. Pandiri, 'Daphnis and Chloe: The Art of Pastoral Play', *Ramus* 14 (1985), 116–41.

J. Bretzigheimer, 'Die Komik in Longos' Hirtenroman "Daphnis und Chloe"', *Gymnasium* 95 (1988), 515–55.

R. Merkelbach, *Die Hirten des Dionysos: Die Dionysos-Mysterien der römischen Kaiserzeit und der bukolische Roman des Longus* (Stuttgart, 1988).

A. Wouters, 'The *Eikones* in Longus' Daphnis and Chloe IV 39,2: "Beglaubigungsapparat"?', *Sacris Erudiri. Jaarboek voor Godsdienstwetenschappen* 31 (1989/90), 465–79.

B. D. MacQueen, *Myth, Rhetoric, and Fiction: A Reading of Longus's Daphnis and Chloe* (Lincoln, Nebr./London, 1990).

J. J. Winkler, 'The Education of Chloe: Hidden Injuries of Sex', in Winkler, *The Constraints of Desire* (New York/London, 1990), 101–26.

F. I. Zeitlin, 'The Poetics of Eros: Nature, Art and Imitation in Longus' *Daphnis and Chloe*', in D. M. Halperin/J. J. Winkler/F. I. Zeitlin (eds), *Before Sexuality: The Construction of Erotic Experience in the Ancient Greek World* (Princeton, 1990), 417–64.

D. Teske, *Der Roman des Longos als Werk der Kunst: Untersuchungen zum Verhältnis von Physis und Techne in 'Daphnis und Chloe'* (Münster, 1991).

W. G. Arnott, 'Longus, Natural History, and Realism', in Tatum, *The Search* (see under 'Ancient prose fiction', p. 110), 199–215.

J. R. Morgan, '*Daphnis and Chloe*: Love's Own Sweet Story' in Morgan/Stoneman, *Greek Fiction* (see under 'The Greek novel', p. 110), 64–79.

B. P. Reardon, '*Muthos ou logos*: Longus's Lesbian Pastorals', in Tatum, *The Search* (see under 'Ancient prose fiction', p. 110), 135–47.

F. I. Zeitlin, 'Gardens of Desire in Longus's *Daphnis and Chloe*: Nature, Art, and Imitation', in Tatum, *The Search* (see under 'Ancient prose fiction', p. 110), 148–70.

Lucian, *True Stories*

J. Bompaire, *Lucien écrivain: imitation et création* (Paris, 1958), 658–73.

K. Reyhl, *Antonios Diogenes* (see under 'Antonius Diogenes', p. 113).

M. Mateuzzi, 'Sviluppi narrativi di giuochi linguistici nella Storia vera di Luciano', *Maia* 27 (1975), 225–9.

G. Anderson, *Studies in Lucian's Comic Fiction* (Leiden, 1976), 1–11.

S. C. Fredericks, 'Lucian's *True History* as SF', *Science Fiction Studies* 3 (1976), 49–60.

W. Fauth, 'Utopische Inseln in den "Wahren Geschichten" des Lukian', *Gymnasium* 86 (1979), 39–58.

J. A. Hall, *Lucian's Satire* (New York, 1981), 338–54.

J. R. Morgan, 'Lucian's *True Histories*' (see under 'Antonius Diogenes', p. 113).

M. Fusillo, 'Le miroir de la Lune: L'*Histoire vraie* de Lucien de la satire à l'utopie', *Poétique* 73 (1988), 109–35.

A. M. Scarcella, 'Mythe et ironie. Les "vraies histoires" de Lucien', in F. Jonan/B. Deforge (eds), *Peuples et pays mythiques. Actes du Ve Colloque du Centre de recherches mythologiques de l'Université de Paris* (Paris, 1988), 169–76.

L. Sciolla, *Gli artifici della finzione poetica nella Storia Vera di Luciano* (Foggia, 1988).

A. Beltrametti, 'Mimesis parodica e parodia della mimesis', in D. Lanza/O. Longo (eds), *Il meraviglioso e il verosimile tra antichità e medioevo* (Firenze, 1989), 211–25.

D. van Mal-Maeder, 'Les détournements homériques dans l'*Histoire vraie* de Lucien: le rapatriement d'une tradition littéraire', *Études de Lettres. Revue de la Faculté des Lettres. Université de Lausanne* (1992), 123–46.

A. Georgiadou/D. H. J. Larmour, 'Lucian and Historiography: "De Historia Conscribenda" and "Verae Historiae"', *Aufstieg und Niedergang der Römischen Welt* ii. 34.2 (1994), 1448–509.

S. Swain, 'Dio and Lucian', in Morgan/Stoneman, *Greek Fiction* (see under 'The Greek novel', p. 110), 166–80.

Ninus

B. E. Perry, *The Ancient Romances* (see under 'The Genre', p. 111), 150–80.

R. Kussl, *Papyrusfragmente* (see under 'Texts': 'Editions of fragments', p. 106), 13–101.

M. Gronewald, 'Zum Ninos-Roman', *Zeitschrift für Papyrologie und Epigraphik* 97 (1993), 1–6.

G. N. Sandy, 'New Pages of Greek Fiction' (see under '*Iolaus*', p. 119).

Parthenope

H. Maehler, 'Der Metiochos-Parthenope-Roman', *Zeitschrift für Papyrologie und Epigraphik* 23 (1976), 1–20.

A. Dihle, 'Zur Datierung des Metiochos-Romans', *Würzburger Jahrbücher für die Altertumswissenschaft* 4 (1978), 47–55.

SELECT BIBLIOGRAPHY

T. Hägg, 'The *Parthenope Romance* Decapitated?', *Symbolae Osloenses* 59 (1984), 61–91.

B. Utas, 'Did ᶜAdhrā Remain a Virgin?', *Orientalia Suecana* 33–5 (1984–6), 429–41.

T. Hägg, 'Metiochus at Polycrates' Court', *Eranos* 83 (1985), 92–102.

T. Hägg, 'The Oriental Reception of Greek Novels: A Survey with Some Preliminary Considerations', *Symbolae Osloenses* 61 (1986), 99–131.

T. Hägg, '*Callirhoe* and *Parthenope*: The Beginnings of the Historical Novel', *Classical Antiquity* 6 (1987), 184–204.

T. Hägg, 'Hermes and the Invention of the Lyre: An Unorthodox Version', *Symbolae Osloenses* 64 (1989), 36–73.

G. N. Sandy, 'New Pages of Greek Fiction' (see under '*Iolaus*', p. 119).

Petronius

R. Heinze, 'Petron und der griechische Roman', *Hermes* 34 (1899), 494–519; also in Gärtner, *Beiträge* (see under 'The Greek novel', p. 110), 15–40.

W. Arrowsmith, 'Luxury and Death in the Satyricon', *Arion* 5 (1966), 304–31; also in N. Rudd (ed.), *Essays on Classical Literature, Selected from Arion* (Cambridge, 1972), 122–45.

J. P. Sullivan, *The Satyricon of Petronius: A Literary Study* (London, 1968).

C. Stöcker, *Humor bei Petron* (doct. diss. University of Erlangen, 1969).

K. F. C. Rose, *The Date and Authorship of the Satyricon* (Leiden, 1971).

F. I. Zeitlin, 'Petronius as Paradox: Anarchy and Artistic Integrity', *Transactions and Proceedings of the American Philological Association* 102 (1971), 631–84.

F. I. Zeitlin, 'Romanus Petronius: A Study of the *Troiae Halosis* and the *Bellum Civile*', *Latomus* 30 (1971), 56–82.

R. Beck, 'Some Observations on the Narrative Technique of Petronius', *Phoenix* 27 (1973), 42–61.

P. A. George, 'Petronius and Lucan *De Bello Civili*', *Classical Quarterly* 68 (1974), 119–33.

R. Beck, 'Encolpius at the *Cena*', *Phoenix* 29 (1975), 271–83.

O. Pecere, *Petronio: la novella della matrona di Efeso* (Padova, 1975).

M. Coffey, *Roman Satire* (London/New York, 1976), 178–203.

K. P. Warren, *Illusion and Reality in the Satyricon* (unpubl. doct. diss. Vanderbilt University, 1976).

R. Astbury, 'Petronius, *P.Oxy.* 3010, and Menippean Satire', *Classical Philology* 72 (1977), 22–31.

F. M. Fröhlke, *Petron, Struktur und Wirklichkeit: Bausteine zu einer Poetik des antiken Romans* (Frankfurt am Main/Bern, 1977).

H. Petersmann, *Petrons urbane Prosa: Untersuchungen zu Sprache und Text (Syntax)* (Wien, 1977).

R. Beck, 'Eumolpus *poeta*, Eumolpus *fabulator*: A Study of Characterization in the *Satyricon*', *Phoenix* 33 (1979), 239–53.

C. W. Müller, 'Die Witwe von Ephesus – Petrons Novelle und die "Milesiaka" des Aristeides', *Antike und Abendland* 26 (1980), 103–21.

R. Beck, 'The Satyricon: Satire, Narrator, and Antecedents', *Museum Helveticum* 39 (1982), 206–214.

P. Fedeli, 'La matrona di Efeso: strutture narrative e tecnica dell'inversione', *Materiali e contributi per la storia della narrativa greco-latina* 4 (1986), 9–35.

R. Herzog, 'Fest, Terror und Tod in Petrons *Satyrica*', in W. Haug/R. Warning (eds), *Das Fest*, Poetik und Hermeneutik 12 (München, 1989), 120–50.

N. Horsfall, '"The Uses of Literacy" and the *Cena Trimalchionis*', *Greece & Rome* 36 (1989), 74–89,194–209.

C. Knight, 'Listening to Encolpius: Modes of Confusion in the *Satyricon*', *University of Toronto Quarterly* 58 (1989), 335–54.

G. Huber, *Das Motiv der 'Witwe von Ephesus' in lateinischen Texten der Antike und des Mittelalters* (Tübingen, 1990).

N. Slater, *Reading Petronius* (Baltimore/London, 1990).

B. Boyce, *The Language of the Freedmen in Petronius' Cena Trimalchionis* (Leiden, 1991).

A. Perutelli, 'Il narratore nel *Satyricon*', *Materiali e discussioni per l'analisi dei testi classici* 25 (1991), 9–25.

J. Bodel, 'Trimalchio's Underworld', in Tatum, *The Search* (see under 'Ancient prose fiction', p. 110), 237–59.

Philostratus, *Life of Apollonius of Tyana*

F. Lo Cascio, *La forma letteraria della Vita di Apollonio Tianeo* (Palermo, 1974).

E. L. Bowie, 'Apollonius of Tyana: Tradition and Reality', *Aufstieg und Niedergang der Römischen Welt* ii. 16.2 (1978), 1652–99.

G. Anderson, *Philostratus: Biography and Belles Lettres in the Third Century AD* (London, 1986).

M. Dzielska, *Apollonius of Tyana in Legend and History* (Roma, 1986).

A. Billault, 'Les formes romanesques de l'héroisation dans la *Vie d'Apollonius de Tyana* de Philostrate', *Bulletin de l'Association Guillaume Budé* (1991), 267–74.

E. Koskenniemi, *Der philostrateische Apollonios* (Helsinki, 1991).

G. Anderson, *Sage, Saint and Sophist: Holy Men and Their Associates in the Early Roman Empire* (London/New York, 1994).

E. Bowie, 'Philostratus: Writer of Fiction', in Morgan/Stoneman, *Greek Fiction* (see 'The Greek novel', p. 110), 181–99.

SELECT BIBLIOGRAPHY

Pseudo-Callisthenes

A. Ausfeld, *Der griechische Alexanderroman*, Herausgegeben von W. Kroll (Leipzig, 1907).

R. Merkelbach, *Die Quellen des griechischen Alexanderromans* (München, 1954; ²1977).

C. Stöcker, 'Der Trug der Olympias: Ein Beitrag zur Erzählkunst antiker Novellistik', *Würzburger Jahrbücher für die Altertumswissenschaft* 2 (1976), 85–98.

F. Pfister, *Kleine Schriften zum Alexanderroman* (Meisenheim, 1976).

A. Cizek, 'Historical Distortions and Saga Patterns in the Pseudo-Callisthenes Romance', *Hermes* 106 (1978), 593–607.

C. Garcia Gual, 'Eléments mythiques et biographie romanesque: la *Vie d'Alexandre* du Pseudo-Callisthène', in C. Calame (ed.), *Métamorphoses du mythe en Grèce antique* (Genève, 1988), 128–38.

S. M. Burstein, 'SEG 33.802 and the Alexander Romance', *Zeitschrift für Papyrologie und Epigraphik* 77 (1989), 275–6.

R. Merkelbach, 'Der Brief des Dareios im Getty-Museum und Alexanders Wortwechsel mit Parmenion', *Zeitschrift für Papyrologie und Epigraphik* 77 (1989), 277–80.

R. Stoneman, 'Oriental Motifs in the Alexander Romance', *Antichthon* 26 (1992), 95–113.

R. Stoneman, 'Romantic Ethnography: Central Asia and India in the *Alexander Romance*', *The Ancient World* 25 (1994), 93–107.

R. Stoneman, 'The *Alexander Romance*: From History to Fiction', in Morgan/Stoneman, *Greek Fiction* (see under 'The Greek novel', p. 110), 117–29.

Pseudo-Clementines

B. Rehm, 'Clemens Romanus 2', *Reallexikon für Antike und Christentum* 3 (1957), 197–206.

B. E. Perry, *The Ancient Romances* (see under 'The genre', p. 111), 285–93.

Sesonchosis

J. N. O'Sullivan/W. A. Beck, 'P.Oxy.3319: The Sesonchosis Romance', *Zeitschrift für Papyrologie und Epigraphik* 45 (1982), 71–83.

J. N. O'Sullivan, 'The Sesonchosis Romance', *Zeitschrift für Papyrologie und Epigraphik* 56 (1984), 39–44.

C. Ruiz-Montero, 'P.Oxy.2466: The Sesonchosis Romance', *Zeitschrift für Papyrologie und Epigraphik* 79 (1989), 51–7.

THE ANCIENT NOVEL

Xenophon of Athens, *Cyropaedia*

B. Due, *The* Cyropaedia: *Xenophon's Aims and Methods* (Aarhus, 1989).

J. Tatum, *Xenophon's Imperial Fiction: On the Education of Cyrus* (Princeton, 1989).

B. Zimmermann, 'Roman und Enkomion – Xenophons "Erziehung des Kyros"', *Würzburger Jahrbücher für die Altertumswissenschaft* 15 (1989), 97–105.

P. Stadter, 'Fictional Narrative in the *Cyropaideia*', *American Journal of Philology* 112 (1991), 461–91.

D. L. Gera, *Xenophon's Cyropaedia: Style, Genre and Literary Technique* (Oxford, 1993).

J. Tatum, 'The Education of Cyrus', in Morgan/Stoneman, *Greek Fiction* (see under 'The Greek novel', p. 110), 15–28.

Xenophon of Ephesus

K. Bürger, 'Zu Xenophon von Ephesus', *Hermes* 27 (1892), 36–67.

F. Zimmermann, 'Die *Ephesiaka* des sog. Xenophon von Ephesos: Untersuchungen zur Technik und Komposition', *Würzburger Jahrbücher für die Altertumswissenschaft* 4 (1949/50), 252–86; also in Gärtner, *Beiträge* (see under 'Ancient prose fiction', p. 110), 295–329.

T. Hägg, 'Die Ephesiaka des Xenophon Ephesios – Original oder Epitome?', *Classica et Mediaevalia* 27 (1966), 118–61.

H. Gärtner, 'Xenophon von Ephesos', *Pauly-Wissowa* ix A 2 (1967), 2055–89.

T. Hägg, 'The Naming of the Characters in the Romance of Xenophon Ephesius', *Eranos* 69 (1971), 25–59.

A. M. Scarcella, 'Les structures socio-économiques du roman de Xénophon d'Éphèse', *Revue des Études Grecques* 90 (1977), 249–62.

J. G. Griffiths, 'Xenophon of Ephesus on Isis and Alexandria', in *Hommages à M. J. Vermaseren*, vol. i (Leiden, 1978), 409–37.

A. M. Scarcella, 'La struttura del romanzo di Senofonte Efesio', *La struttura della fabulazione antica* (Genova, 1979), 89–113.

G. L. Schmeling, *Xenophon of Ephesus* (Boston, Mass., 1980).

F. Sartori, 'Italie et Sicilie dans le roman de Xénophon d'Éphèse', *Journal des Savants* (1985), 161–86.

D. Konstan, 'Xenophon of Ephesus: Eros and Narrative in the Novel', in Morgan/Stoneman, *Greek Fiction* (see under 'The Greek novel', p. 110), 49–63.

C. Ruiz Montero, 'Xenophon von Ephesos: Ein Überblick', *Aufstieg und Niedergang der Römischen Welt* ii. 34.2 (1994), 1088–138.

INDEX

INDEX

Iamblichus, *Babyloniaca* 7, 18, 45, 84, 85–7
Iambulus 12–14, 17
Iliad 48
Iolaus 7, 11, 63, 64
Isis 4, 5, 6, 30, 54, 73, 79, 80, 82

Julian 37, 104
Julius Valerius 17

language and style 53, 54, 66, 84, 102–3
Letters of Aeschines 19
Letters of Alexander the Great 19
Letters of Chion 19, 20
Letters of Euripides 19
Letters of Hippocrates 19, 20
Letters of Phalaris 19–20
Letters of Plato 19
Letters of the Seven Wise Men 19
Letters of Socrates and the Socratics 19
Letters of Themistocles 19
Life of Aesop 15–16, 17
Lollianus, *Phoenicica* 7, 54–6, 57, 86
Longus, *Daphnis and Chloe* 6, 84, 93–9, 103
Lucian 76–7; *True Stories* 14, 76
Lucius of Patrae 73, 75, 76, 85

Marini, N. 51
Menander 8, 32
Menippean satire 62, 64
Merkelbach, R. 19, 30–1, 56
motifs 2, 9–10, 11, 12, 15, 18, 22, 24, 25, 40, 44, 50, 51–2, 53, 56, 67–8, 76, 88, 93, 94, 95, 102

narrative technique 10–11, 45, 46, 58, 77–8, 90–1, 99–100, 102–3; *see also* first-person narrative
Nicephorus Callistus 104
Ninus 7, 14, 21, 34, 36, 37, 38–9, 40, 41, 45
novel: ancient labels 8–9; and comedy 8–9, 10–11, 32–3, 45, 46, 95; definition of 26–7; digressions in 10, 18, 36, 86–7,

91; and epic 10, 33, 48, 64; and historiography 10, 35–42, 46–7, 50–1; ideological framework for 11, 18–19, 23, 30–1, 54, 70, 103; mosaics illustrating 34, 39, 50; parody in 7–8, 22, 61–2, 64, 67–8, 75; satire in 72, 77, 78, 82; social-political background of 28–9, 30–3; transmission of 6–7, 16–17, 43, 50, 64–5, 87

Odyssey 48, 70
O'Sullivan, J. 40
Ovid, *Ars amatoria* 92, 98

papyri 25, 38, 40, 49, 50, 51, 54, 58, 63, 91; *see also* novel, transmission of
Parthenope 7, 34, 36, 47, 48–50, 53, 64, 66
Perry, B. E. 29–30
Persius, *Satires* 43
Petronius, *Satyrica* 7, 11, 16, 17, 20, 22, 55, 61–2, 63–72, 75, 76, 77, 87, 90, 99, 105
Philostratus, *Life of Apollonius of Tyana* 18–19, 59, 103
Photius 57, 58, 60, 73, 76, 85, 86, 87
picaresque novel 16, 17, 61, 63, 76
Plato 20, 83; *Phaedrus* 81–2; *Symposium* 49, 66; *see also* *Letters of Plato*
Priapus 64, 65
Pseudo-Callisthenes, *Alexander Romance* 17–18, 22, 37, 41, 45
Pseudo-Clementines see Clement Romance
Pseudo-Lucian, *Lucius or the Ass see Ass Romance*

readership 33–5
Reardon, B. 95
Rohde, E. 28, 29, 46, 52, 92
Rufinus of Aquileia 24

Second Sophistic 83, 84–5, 91, 94, 102